Homestyle INDIAN Cooking

BY
PAT CHAPMAN

THE CROSSING PRESS
FREEDOM, CALIFORNIA

Copyright © 1998 by Pat Chapman
Cover design by Victoria May
Photographs by B.E. International Ltd.
Printed in the U.S.A.

First published in 1988 by Judy Piatkus (Publishers) Ltd., London.

For information on bulk purchases or group discounts for this and other Crossing Press titles, please contact our Special Sales Manager at 800-777-1048 Ext.214.

Visit our Web site on the Internet: www.crossingpress.com

Library of Congress Cataloging-in-Publication Data

Chapman, Pat, 1940-
   Homestyle Indian cooking / by Pat Chapman.
      p. cm. – (Homestyle cooking series)
   Includes index.
   ISBN 0-89594-923-7 (pbk.)
   1. Cookery, Indic. I. Title. II. Series.
TX724.5.I4C3755 1998
641.5954–dc21
                                    98-26029
                                        CIP

CONTENTS

USEFUL INFORMATION

KITCHEN EQUIPMENT

In the recipes that follow, you will need a frying pan, a broiler pan and rack, two or three saucepans, the largest of which should hold 3 quarts and measure about 8 inches in diameter and 5 inches deep. You will also need one or more lidded casserole dishes of between 2- and 3-quart capacity, and ordinary oven baking trays. You need large and small mixing bowls, measuring equipment, sharp knives, and a rolling pin and board.

Two special Indian cooking pans that I find extremely useful are the *karahi* or *kadahi* and the *tawa* or *tava*. The *karahi* is the Indian version of the Chinese wok. Traditionally it is made of cast iron, has two handles and a rounded bottom for use over charcoal fires. Modern *karahis* are made from pressed carbon steel and the bottom is flattened to enable the pan to be used on modern stoves. The *karahi* is an all-purpose cooking pan used for stir-frying, simmering, frying, and deep-frying. Its hemispherical shape makes it efficient in a way that a conventional frying pan or saucepan is not. The heat is at its hottest on the flat part and it then gets progressively cooler the higher up the sides you go. This enables the cook to control the temperature of the ingredients by shifting them from the center outwards. It's shape makes it very efficient for deep-frying.

The new-style food processor purées just about anything, without liquid, and is particularly good for garlic, ginger, and onion. I also find it perfect for grinding meat for kebabs. It achieves the fine pounded texture akin to the authentic stone-pounded technique, especially when fresh garlic, ginger, coriander, hot pepper, and spices are thrown in, too. The difference is that the processor does in sixty seconds what the Indian villager would need sixty minutes' hard labor to do.

Other useful tools include electric deep-fryers, crockpots, rice cookers, and yogurt makers. Electric coffee grinders manage to grind most spices in small doses.

SPICES

Spices are vegetable matter. Most are seeds, pods, or berries, while others are dry leaves, stigma, buds, roots, rhizomes, even resin. They are harvested from trees, shrubs, plants, or flowers.

Most spices taken on their own are bitter, unpalatable, and, in some cases, inedible (cassia or cinnamon bark for example), but used correctly in small amounts, singly or in combination, they add flavor to the food. There are more than sixty whole spices that can be used in Indian cooking. Fortunately some of these are rarely used, while some are virtually indispensable. Some are used whole, some ground.

Storing Spices

Whole spices retain their flavor longer than ground, for one year or more sometimes. Ground spices give off a stronger aroma than whole, and of course this means their storage life is that much shorter. Three months is about right for most ground items. So plan your larder accordingly, and buy little and often and grind freshly. Keep the spices out of sunlight (a dark pantry is best) and in airtight, labeled containers.

Grinding Spices

It is better by far to grind your own whole spices whenever you can. First, you can be sure of the quality and contents, and second, they will be fresher and tastier. The traditional method is by mortar and pestle, but you can use an electric coffee grinder or spice mill. After a damp wipe, a coffee grinder can still be used for coffee—it might even enhance the flavor! Use small quantities to prevent overloading the motor.

Don't try to grind dry ginger or turmeric. They are too fibrous for most small grinders, and commercial powders are adequate. Peppers—cayenne, paprika, and black or white pepper—are tricky, and commercially ground peppers will suffice. The oilier spices (cloves, nutmeg, brown cardamom, and bay leaves) are easier to grind if roasted first.

In the recipes, when a spice is referred to as ground, this means factory ground. Where it requires the spice to be home ground (usually after roasting), the recipe clearly states this.

Roasting Spices

Whole spices are roasted to enhance or change the flavor. The roasting can be done in a dry pan on the stove, in a dry electric frying pan, under the broiler, or in the oven. Each spice should be heated until it gives off an aroma. The heat should be medium rather than hot and the time required is a few minutes. The spice should not blacken, a light brown at most is sufficient. The original oil of the spice must not be totally cooked or it will lose its flavor. A little experimenting will soon show you how to do it. In some recipes pre-roasted spices are important.

HERBS

Herbs also add flavor to food. They also add greatly to the appearance of a dish when used as garnishes. It is surprising that the use of herbs in Indian cooking is minimal. In fact, the main herb is cilantro, which has a very distinctive musky flavor. It contributes greatly to achieving authentic flavors.

The other herb that is used from time to time is mint, particularly spearmint. I use it in a few of the recipes. A tiny pinch of dried mint livens up many curry dishes, giving them a fresh flavor. Add it 10 minutes before the end of cooking.

SELECTED CURRY INGREDIENTS

Certain ingredients are used to add texture and/or flavor to Indian cooking, chief of which are garlic, ginger, onion, coconut, hot peppers, oils, and dairy products.

Coconut

Coconut is used extensively in South India and Bengal and all the curry lands to the East. Flaked coconut is one substitute for fresh coconut and can be used by adding it dry to your cooking, or by simmering it in water and straining it to create coconut milk.

To choose a fresh coconut, shake before buying to ensure it is full of liquid (the more liquid it has, the fresher it is). Coconuts without liquid or with moldy or wet eyes should not be used.

To prepare coconut:

- Make a hole in two of the three eyes with a screwdriver or nail. Drain off and keep the liquid (coconut water).
- Bake the empty coconut in the oven at 400°F for 15 minutes.
- While still hot, crack it with a hammer. Remove the flesh.
- Cut into 1-inch cubes and soak in water for 4 hours.
- Strain the flesh, reserving the liquid.
- Squeeze the flesh to get the remaining liquid.
- Combine all the liquids to make coconut milk.

Use the flesh in chunks or puréed in curries.

Oils and Ghee

Curry cooking depends very greatly on the use of oil to establish both flavor and texture, particularly in the early stages of cooking. And there is no argument that using *more* oil creates a better curry than using less. There is a limit to this, of course. We are all probably familiar with curries served at restaurants swimming in oil. In such a case, too much oil was used in the first place, and no matter how good the end result, the excess oil spoils the dish. It could so easily have been spooned off at the end of its cooking while still in the saucepan. Once a properly cooked curry is taken off direct heat and allowed to rest, all the oil rises to the top and can then be ladled off for future use in curry cooking.

Oils are extensively used in southern India. Those described as polyunsaturated are said to be better and these include certain vegetable oils, such as sunflower and soy oil. Best of all are said to be monounsaturated oils which include peanut, canola, and olive oil.

Peanut and canola are excellent for curry cooking, but olive oil has too strong a flavor.

In many dishes the oil used affects the final taste very minimally, so most oils can be used instead of ghee. But in rice and bread cooking, ghee imparts an important flavor. I have tried to strike a happy balance in these recipes by specifying neither too much nor too little ghee or oil. You can always use more if that is to your taste, but remember to spoon off excess before serving.

Dairy Items

Indians are great milk consumers. They use the milk of cows, buffalo, and goats. They make cream and yogurt, but cheese isn't traditional. Indian cheese (paneer) is a simple form of cottage cheese.

Yogurt is easy to make at home. Yogurt is ordinary milk that has been fermented by means of heat and a starter bacteria (usually other yogurt).

Condensed milk is used in Indian sweets and is made by continually stirring milk until it reduces to a thick texture.

Some Indian restaurant chefs use ordinary milk as a cooking ingredient in curry. It reduces to a nice thick sauce, and when it is added to curries with slightly acidic ingredients (tomatoes or vinegar, for example) the milk can "curdle," i.e., turn into curds and whey, but this is not an unpleasant effect; the curds are minute and virtually tasteless.

Evaporated milk can be used to obtain a creamy taste in kormas, etc.

CHEMICALS IN FOOD

Spices are used in Indian cooking primarily to enhance the flavor of the principal ingredients. They also affect the color of the dish. Turmeric is used to give yellows; coriander, cumin, clove, etc. for shades of brown;

paprika and cayenne powder for red; fresh cilantro and hot pepper for green. Saffron, the world's most expensive spice, gives a bright orangey-gold color, and deep crimson is obtained by use of *ratan jot* (a plant in the borage family). Natural colors such as these have been used in the subcontinent for as long as anyone can remember.

It took the latter half of the twentieth century and food factories to forget the old ways. In the interests of time and cost saving, chemicals have crept into so many Western food products that I haven't space to mention them. Not surprisingly, chemical technology has crept into Indian food as well.

Nowhere is this more apparent than in the tandoori/tikka department. Those bright orangy-red chunks of chicken and lamb look so attractive on their beds of lettuce, onion rings, and lemon wedges, but it's all, quite frankly, baloney. The authentic dish in the Punjab, from where this style of cooking originated, looks pale and anemic in its natural un-dyed state but is, of course, just as tasty, for these chemicals are quite tasteless.

I am not emotional about the use of chemical coloring in food. I am not allergic to them, but like everyone else, including the manufacturers, I don't know what, if any, their cumulative effect is. I listen to the contemporary debate and I feel the manufacturers should listen, too. My conclusion is that when I cook for the public I must do without chemicals, so I set about looking for alternatives. I found beet powder to be a substitute for the deep red color and annatto seed powder works for yellow. Combinations of these work well for tandoori.

KEEPING CURRIES

I find two schools of thought about curry. One is that it should be cooked and served fresh, the other that it is better left for a day or two to marinate.

Keeping a fresh curry in the refrigerator overnight is safe. Provided that the raw ingredients are absolutely fresh, not frozen, and are cooked immediately, and provided that the dish is cooled rapidly after cooking, covered, and placed in the refrigerator at once, then it will be safe for up to 48 hours.

- Do not keep fish or shellfish curries in this way.
- If you intend to keep a curry for a day or two, cut back on the cooking time by 10 minutes. You will obtain a better texture when reheating—simply simmer until ready.
- Use common sense about which vegetables will keep.
- Inspect meat or chicken after 24 hours. Smell and taste it. It should look firm.
- Ensure that when the curry is reheated it simmers for at least 10 minutes.
- During reheating, taste, and if it needs a boost of a little more spicing, add them early so that they cook in well.

Freezing Curries

Curries freeze as well as any other dish.
- Use only fresh ingredients.
- Some ingredients are not suitable for freezing—their texture is unpleasant when thawed, for instance. Meat and poultry are excellent, as are all lentil dishes. Some vegetables work well—eggplant, peas, beans, carrots—while others don't—potato, okra, zucchini, etc. Fish and seafood work well. Rice is satisfactory but I never see the point—it takes less time to make fresh rice (and it has better taste and texture).
- Always undercook a dish destined for the freezer by about 10 minutes to allow for "tenderizing" in the freezing and reheating process.
- Take out any large whole spices before freezing, especially cinnamon stick, cardamoms, and cloves as they tend become a bit astringent in flavor.

- Get the dish into the freezer as soon as you can once it is cool.
- Be aware that spicy food can taint other foods, so preferably pack in a plastic container with an airtight lid.
- Label with contents and date.
- Use within 3 months.
- When reheating, ensure that the dish is thoroughly hot and cooked through.
- You may find the spicing has become a little bland, so taste and add more spices as needed.

STOCKING THE PANTRY

Here is a workable list of items you need in your cupboard to make the recipes in this book. I have subdivided them into essential and nonessential. The essential items appear again and again in the recipes, the nonessential appear in only one or two. Before you start cooking, check your supplies. Nothing guarantees putting you off a cookbook more than finding you don't have an ingredient. This list may look a bit formidable but remember once you have the items in stock they will last for some time.

Essential Whole Spices

Bay leaves
Cardamom, black or brown
Cardamom, green or white
Cassia bark
Cloves
Coriander seeds
Cumin seeds, white
Curry leaves, dry
Dried hot peppers
Fennel seeds
Fenugreek leaves, dry
Mustard seeds
Peppercorns, black
Sesame seeds
Wild onion seeds

Essential Ground Spices

Black pepper
Coriander
Cumin
Garam masala
Garlic powder
Ginger
Ground red pepper (cayenne)
Paprika
Turmeric

Nonessential Whole Spices

Alkenet root
Cinnamon bark
Cumin seeds, black
Dill seeds
Fenugreek seeds
Ginger, dried
Lovage seeds
Mace
Nutmeg, whole
Panch phoran
Pomegranate seeds
Poppy seeds
Saffron stamens

Nonessential Ground Spices

Asafoetida
Cardamom, green
Cassia bark
Cloves
Mango powder

Essential Dry Foods

Basmati rice
Flaked coconut
Chickpea flour
Masoor (red) lentils

Nonessential Dry Foods

Bombay duck
Food coloring powder, red
Food coloring powder, yellow
Lentils—*Channa*, split
   Moong green, whole
   Toor or *tovar*, split
   Urid, whole black
Nuts—Almond, whole
   Almond, ground
   Cashew
   Peanuts, raw
   Pistachio

Pappadams, spiced and plain
Puffed rice (*mamra*)
Red kidney beans
Rice flour
Rosewater, bottle
Silver leaf (edible)
Supari mixture
Tamarind block

CURRY BASES
AND BASICS

▲▲▲▲▲▲▲▲▲▲▲▲▲▲▲▲▲

In my view, this is the most important chapter in the book for the cook who is aiming to capture authentic flavor. Here you will find recipes that deal specifically with the cooking of spices and curry bases. These recipes are referred to throughout the book.

You can make the same curry in a number of different ways. For example, you may wish to use a mixture of dry spices (such as the following curry powder) made into a paste and fried, or you may wish to use a premade paste. You might prefer to use garlic, ginger, or onion purée on one occasion, whereas you might like to chop them and fry them unpuréed on another. Alternatively, you might choose to use the curry-masala-sauce technique from page 22. You will find that you can use alternative curry-base methods from this chapter at the initial cooking stages to achieve the same end result. It is impractical to state this in all the recipes—it would take up too much space—but I do hope you will simply use the recipes as a guide, either following them precisely, or taking an alternative route, using shortcuts or making changes as the mood takes you.

Whichever way you set about cooking curry, remember that the most important factor is to maintain a correct texture—thick and creamy. Maintaining a good balance between oil and water is the key to obtaining the desired result. Apart from that observation, there is no reason at all why you should not be completely flexible in your approach.

Mild Curry Powder

YIELDS
4 CUPS

Commercial curry powder has two drawbacks in my view. First, although the manufacturers are supposed to list the ingredients, some avoid it by simply stating "spices"; and even if they do list them, they do not state the quantities. They often put in too much cayenne, salt, and in some cases, chemical colorings and preservatives. Undeclared additives can include husks and stalks and other adulterations.

The second drawback is that the use of the same curry powder blend in all the recipes would make each dish taste virtually the same.

However, it is sometimes useful to have curry powder in the pantry. You can purchase a commercial version or you can make up your own with this interesting mixture. It comes from the first cookbook given to a young bride who, with her husband, was posted to the British army base in Agra in 1904. The lady was my grandmother and that book was her bible. It was first published in 1870, so this curry powder has been recipe tested for 125 years.

There are several ways of utilizing the spices and flavorings for curry making. The first stage is the mixing together of the ground spices, the masala—the unique combination that makes Indian-style cooking so distinctive. The following curry powder recipe is a masala, but throughout the recipes I refer to the masala as **Spices** (whole or ground).

As the spices need to be cooked slightly to get rid of raw flavors, the next step is to make them into a paste with a little water. The cooking can be done by simply adding the powder to hot oil (many restaurant cooks do this), but it is very easy to burn the spices this way, and a paste is safer. The cooking of the masala—the *bhoona*—is the next stage.

The cooking of whole spices as opposed to ground—the *bargar*—is another technique which I outline, as is the puréeing and cooking of onion, ginger, garlic, and cilantro.

INGREDIENTS

1 1/4 cups coriander seeds	1 tablespoon dry ground curry leaves
1/2 cup white cumin seeds	1 tablespoon asafoetida
2 tablespoons fenugreek seeds	1 tablespoon ground ginger
5 tablespoons chickpea flour (*besan*)	1 tablespoon ground red pepper (cayenne)
6 tablespoons garlic powder	1 tablespoon yellow mustard powder
5 tablespoons paprika	1 tablespoon ground black pepper
5 tablespoons turmeric	
5 tablespoons aromatic Garam Masala (storebought or homemade, see page 35)	

METHOD

- Roast and then grind the first three spices.

- Mix these and all the rest together well and store.

- Omit the final four spices for a totally mild curry powder.

- For those who wish, salt and sugar (white granulated) can be added during the blending: add 2 tablespoons sugar and/or 1 teaspoon salt.

To make a dish for four you would need about 6 tablespoons of curry powder, so this will give you 10 portions. I prefer to make a reasonable batch like 4 cups because it matures or becomes better blended the longer it is stored. It can be used at once, of course, but after about a month it is perfect. Do not keep it for longer than 18 months—it tends to lose its subtle flavors, becoming bitter. Store in an airtight container in a dark, damp-free place.

The Masala Paste

When a recipe states "mix and blend dry spices" (a masala), such as in the previous curry powder mixture, it is necessary to cook those spices to remove the raw flavors. This is most safely done by making up a paste with water to obtain a thick texture. The water prevents the spices from burning up when they are introduced to the oil in the *bhoona*, or frying process.

METHOD

- Select a mixing bowl large enough to enable you to stir the masala.

- Stir the masala until it is fully mixed.

- Add enough water and *no more* to form a stiff paste.

- Let stand for a minimum of 10 minutes. It does not matter how *long* it stands. This ensures that the ground spices absorb all the water.

- Add a little water if it is too dry before using in the frying process.

The Bhoona

The *bhoona* Hindi term for the process of cooking the spice paste in hot oil. This is an important part of the curry cooking process that removes the raw taste of the spices and influences the final taste of the dish. Use the *bhoona* method whenever the recipes in this book state that you should "fry the spices." Traditionally the spice paste is fried first, then the puréed or chopped onion is added. This method can easily cause burned spices so I reverse this process and have found that it works very satisfactorily.

METHOD

■ Take a round-sided pan such as a *karahi* or wok. If you don't have one, use an ordinary frying pan (a nonstick one is best).

■ Heat the oil to quite a high heat (but not smoking).

■ Remove the pan from the heat and at once gently add the onion purée. Return to the heat and begin stirring.

■ *From this point do not let your attention wander.* Keep stirring the purée until the oil is hot again, then gently add the masala paste. Beware of splattering.

■ Keep stirring. The water in the paste lowers the temperature. Do not let the mixture stick at all. Do not stop stirring, not even for a few seconds.

■ After a few minutes, the water will have evaporated out and the oil will float above the mixture. The spices will be cooked. Remove the pan from the heat. Proceed with the remainder of the recipe.

The Bargar

Some of the recipes in this book require you to fry whole spices. The need for this is the same as for the *bhoona*—to cook out the raw flavor from the spices. Again the oil should be hot, and the spices are put into the oil with no water or purée. You must use your judgment as to when they are cooked. Do not let them blacken. As soon as they begin to change color or to float, they are ready. It will not take more than a couple of minutes.

If you do burn the *bhoona* or *bargar* you must throw it away and start again. Better to waste a few spices than taint a whole meal.

The Purée

The importance of the purée cannot be overstated, and it is the way to achieve that gorgeous creamy texture. It is based on tradition, of course. In the Indian home the purée is made the hard way by wet-grinding the spices with garlic and/or ginger and/or onion to a fine texture, and it is time-consuming and messy. We are fortunate to have electric blenders and food processors to do the job in seconds. I have heard a purist school of thought that says metal blades taint the items being ground, but it is just not so.

I have given large quantities for each of these purées as it saves time, odors, and washing up. Make large batches, then freeze the surplus in ice-cube molds or empty yogurt containers.

Garlic Purée

YIELDS 10
(3 TEASPOON)
PORTIONS

I still use garlic powder from time to time, but it contains flour and leaves a distinctive flavor. An expensive (but good) product is garlic purée in tubes. A product I have used a lot recently is dehydrated garlic flakes: To use, soak in an equal volume of water for 30 minutes, then blend in a food processor or blender. The flavor is nearly as good as fresh garlic, and the texture is indistinguishable.

One plump clove of garlic is the equivalent of 1 level teaspoon garlic purée. An ice cube container holds about 3 teaspoons of purée.

INGREDIENTS

30 plump garlic cloves, peeled

METHOD

■ Purée the garlic cloves in a blender or food processor, adding no water, or a minimum amount. Scrape the garlic purée out of container, place in 10 ice-cube molds, and freeze.

Ginger Purée

YIELDS 10
(3 TEASPOON)
PORTIONS

Most people think that ginger has to be peeled before using. But I started to experiment and I have found that if ginger is puréed it does not cause bitterness if the skin is left on. Remove the really rough ends or dirty bits, but leave any nice pink skin. It saves a great deal of time.

INGREDIENTS

1 pound fresh ginger, trimmed of hard
   knobs but unpeeled

METHOD

■ Coarsely chop the ginger, then purée in a blender or food processor. Scrape out of container, place in 10 ice-cube molds and freeze raw.

Onion Purée

YIELDS 10
(1/2 CUP)
PORTIONS

Onions do not freeze whole at all well, as they are very watery. They become soggy when they thaw, which is fine for boiling and subsequent puréeing, but of no use if you want to chop and fry them. Raw chopped and puréed onion freezes and thaws satisfactorily.

Unlike garlic and ginger, I find that onion needs to be boiled (blanched) in hot water first before puréeing, otherwise it has a very bitter flavor.

INGREDIENTS

10 Spanish onions, about 8 ounces each,
 peeled

METHOD

■ Coarsely chop the onions, and place them in boiling water. Strain after 3 minutes.

■ Purée in a blender or food processor until very fine in texture.

■ Scrape out of container, place in containers, and freeze.

Cilantro Purée

YIELDS ABOUT 10 (3 TEASPOON PORTIONS)

Cilantro, or fresh coriander, is an essential ingredient for curry, contributing greatly to its flavor. This purée retains the original flavor of cilantro, almost as well as if it were fresh. As with all my purées, I like to make up a large quantity, then freeze it in ice-cube containers, transferring the cubes to a rigid container later. Each cube gives enough cilantro for an average recipe for four.

INGREDIENTS

4 bunches cilantro, washed and trimmed of coarse stalks

1/2 Spanish onion, peeled

METHOD

- Chop the cilantro coarsely, including the smaller stalks. Also chop the onion.

- Put both into a food processor and purée.

- Scrape out and freeze in ice-cube trays.

An alternative to this purée method is simply to chop fresh cilantro, dry it if necessary on paper towels, and freeze.

Curry Pastes and Sauce

Anyone interested in Indian food must have encountered bottled curry pastes on the grocery shelves. There are many makes and types, but little explanation as to what they are or what they do. They are designed to take the labor out of blending a spice mixture, making it into a water paste and frying it. The manufacturers do it all for you, adding vinegar (acetic acid) and hot oil to prevent it from going moldy. Unfortunately, they also add salt and cayenne, which makes them a little overpowering. They are very concentrated, and you only need a small quantity for cooking.

Curry pastes are already cooked, but to disguise them you will probably need to add some other whole or ground spices, and you will certainly need to fry garlic, ginger, onion, etc. Simply add the spice paste after these three are fried and carry on with the rest of the recipe.

Homemade Bottled Curry Paste

**YIELDS
6 CUPS**

The recipe below is for a mild paste which can form the base for many curry dishes. The quantities here will make a reasonable amount. Using vinegar (rather than all water) to make the paste will enable you to preserve it in jars. As with all canning, sterilize the jars (a good hot wash in the dishwasher followed by drying in a low-heat oven will do). Top off the paste in the jar with hot oil and inspect after a few days to see that there is no mold.

INGREDIENTS

Recipe Mild Curry Powder (see page 12)

3/4–1 cup any vinegar

3/4–1 cup vegetable oil

METHOD

■ Mix together the curry powder spices.

■ Add the vinegar and enough water to make a creamy paste.

■ Heat the oil in a wok or *karahi*.

■ Add the paste to the oil. It will splatter a bit so be careful.

■ Stir-fry the paste continually to prevent it sticking until the water content is cooked out (it should take about 5 minutes). As the liquid is reduced, the paste begins to make a regular bubbling noise (hard to describe but it goes chup-chup-chup-chup) if you don't stir, and it will splatter. This is your audible cue that it is ready. You can tell if the spices are cooked by taking the *karahi* off the stove. Let stand for 3–4 minutes. If the oil floats to the top, the spices are cooked. If not add a little more oil and cook for another 5 minutes.

■ Bottle the paste in sterilized jam jars.

■ Heat up a little more oil and top off the paste, by pouring in enough oil to cover the paste. Seal the jars and store.

Green Masala Paste

YIELDS ABOUT 2 1/2 CUPS

This is a kind of curry paste and it is green in color because of its use of cilantro and mint. You can buy it factory made, but it does not have the delicious fresh taste of this recipe from Ivan Wilson, journalist and regular correspondent to *The Curry Magazine*. You will come across green masala paste in the Indian home where it is used to enhance curry dishes and impart a subtle flavor that can be obtained in no other way.

I have not specified its use in many of the following recipes, but you can add a heaped teaspoon in place of fresh cilantro or garam masala towards the end of cooking virtually any dish. Try it on its own with potatoes: Boil potatoes, add 1–1 1/2 tablespoons of green masala paste, stir-fry, and serve.

As with all curry pastes, this one will keep in jars indefinitely if made correctly.

INGREDIENTS

1 teaspoon fenugreek seeds	3 teaspoons turmeric
6 garlic cloves, chopped	2 teaspoons ground red pepper (cayenne)
2 tablespoons finely chopped fresh ginger	1/2 teaspoon ground cloves
1 1/2 cups fresh mint leaves	1 teaspoon ground cardamom seeds
1 1/2 cups fresh cilantro leaves	1/2 cup vegetable oil
1/2 cup vinegar	1/4 cup sesame oil
3 teaspoons salt	

METHOD

■ Soak and fenugreek seeds in water overnight. They will swell and acquire a jelly-like coating.

■ Strain the fenugreek, discarding the water.

■ Process all the ingredients, except the oils, in a blender or food processor, to make a purée.

■ To cook and store, follow the previous curry paste method.

Curry Masala Sauce

YIELDS ABOUT 7 CUPS

Every curry restaurant has a large saucepan on the stove. In it is a pale orangey-gold sauce, quite thick in texture like applesauce. Taste and it's quite nice—a bit like soup—or mild curry. Ask how it's made and like as not you'll get a shake of the head and a murmur about secrets of the trade, for this stockpot is one of the keys to achieving the restaurant's curry. Recipes vary only slightly from chef to chef and restaurant to restaurant.

You can substitute this curry sauce for the individual garlic, ginger, or onion purées given in many of the recipes that follow. Remember, this is just a mild base to which you can add other spices as required.

INGREDIENTS

1 1/4 cups ghee or vegetable oil
5 tablespoons Garlic Purée (see page 16)
4 tablespoons Ginger Purée (see page 16)
1 full recipe Onion Purée (see page 17)
6 tablespoons tomato purée
1 teaspoon salt

SPICES

2 tablespoons turmeric
4 tablespoons Mild Curry Powder (store-bought or homemade, see page 12)
1–6 teaspoons ground red pepper (cayenne) (to taste)
2 tablespoons ground cumin seeds
2 tablespoons finely chopped fresh cilantro leaves

METHOD

■ Mix the **Spices** with water to make a paste that has the approximate consistency of tomato ketchup.

■ Heat the oil. Stir-fry the garlic purée for 3 minutes, then add the ginger purée and cook for 3 more minutes. Add the spice paste and stir-fry until the water has evaporated and the oil separates, about 5 minutes. Should it need it, add enough water to make the sauce pourable.

■ Add the onion purée and stir-fry for another 10 minutes. Then add the tomato purée and stir-fry for a final 10 minutes. Add the salt.

■ Place into 10 containers and freeze.

■ Makes enough sauce for 10 curries (40 portions).

Akhni Stock

**YIELDS
3 1/2 CUPS**

Some restaurants make a strained stock as well as, or in place of, the previous curry masala sauce. This flavored clear liquid, sometimes called *yakhni*, is used exactly like any vegetable stock at any time the recipe says to add water. You can keep it in the refrigerator for a couple of days, but it is essential to re-boil it after this time; it will be safe for several re-boils, but use it finally in a soup or other cooking. Add the brine or water from canned vegetables to your stock. You can top it up with fresh or leftover ingredients as required.

INGREDIENTS

7 cups water	
2 Spanish onions, peeled and chopped	
1 teaspoon Garlic Purée (see page 16)	
1 teaspoon Ginger Purée (see page 16)	
1 tablespoon ghee	
2 teaspoons salt	

SPICES (WHOLE)

10 cloves
10 green cardamoms
6 pieces cassia bark or cinnamon sticks
6 bay leaves

METHOD

- Boil the water, then add everything else.

- Simmer for 1 hour with the lid on, by which time the stock should have reduced by half.

- Strain and discard the solids.

- If you like, add 8 ounces of meat and bones in addition to the other ingredients.

Curry Bases

Every restaurant is able, very quickly, to make up curry dishes at different heat strengths by using their curry masala sauce, spices, and/or paste, and by adding their pre-cooked main ingredients. Hey, presto, the instant curry. The technique varies little from restaurant to restaurant, and it is useful for us to understand it and use it if we wish.

However, when we do have the time and inclination to produce individual curries with distinctive flavors, the best way is to cook them in more conventional ways as indicated in the recipes beginning at chapter 3. Meanwhile, here are the tricks of the trade.

Once you have made your curry base, add the meat, chicken, vegetable or seafood of your choice.

Mild Curry Base

SERVES 4

INGREDIENTS

2 tablespoons ghee or vegetable oil	1 1/4–1 3/4 cups Curry Masala Sauce (see page 22)
1 teaspoon Garlic Purée (see page 16)	2 teaspoons tomato purée
1 tablespoon Curry Paste (storebought or homemade, see page 20), or Mild Curry Powder (storebought or homemade, see page 12)	1 teaspoon salt
	Akhni Stock (see page 23) or water

METHOD

■ Heat the ghee, and stir-fry the garlic purée for 1 minute.

■ Add the curry paste (or powder made into water paste), and stir-fry for 2 more minutes.

■ Add the curry masala sauce, using less if you want a dry curry and more for a liquid sauce. Stir-fry for a couple of minutes, then add the tomato purée and salt.

■ To obtain the correct consistency, either add akhni stock or water to taste. (You may need to add a little oil as well to keep the correct texture.)

■ Add your principal ingredient—1 1/2 pounds meat, chicken, seafood, or vegetables for 4 people—and when hot, serve.

Medium Curry Base

SERVES 4

INGREDIENTS

2 tablespoons ghee or vegetable oil

1 teaspoon Garlic Purée (see page 16)

1/2 teaspoon turmeric

1/2 teaspoon ground red pepper (cayenne)

1 teaspoon aromatic Garam Masala (storebought or homemade, see page 35)

1 tablespoon Curry Paste (storebought or see page 20), or Mild Curry Powder (storebought or homemade, see page 12)

1 1/4–1 3/4 cups Curry Masala Sauce (see page 22)

2 teaspoons tomato purée

Akhni Stock (see page 23) or water

METHOD

■ Heat the ghee, and stir-fry the garlic purée for 1 minute.

■ Add the turmeric, red pepper, and Garam Masala. Stir-fry for 1 minute, then add the curry paste and stir-fry for 2 more minutes.

■ Add the curry masala sauce, using less if you want a dry curry and more for a liquid sauce. Stir-fry for a couple of minutes, then add the tomato purée and salt.

■ To obtain the correct consistency, either add akhni stock or water to taste. (You may need to add a little oil as well to keep the correct texture.)

■ Add your principal ingredient—1 1/2 pounds meat, chicken, seafood, or vegetables for 4 people—and when hot, serve.

Madras Curry Base

SERVES 4

The Madras curry is the standard hot, slightly sour curry found in many Indian restaurants. In reality there is no such dish as this in Madras (the largest city in southern India), and you won't find its recipe in any cookbook containing authentic recipes. But it is a very tasty dish if you enjoy a bit of a "kick" with your food.

INGREDIENTS

2 tablespoons ghee or vegetable oil

1 teaspoon Garlic Purée (see page 16)

1/2 teaspoon turmeric

1/2 teaspoon ground cumin

1 teaspoon ground black pepper

1 teaspoon ground red pepper (cayenne)

1/2 Spanish onion, peeled and thinly sliced

1 tablespoon Curry Paste (storebought or homemade, see page 20) or Mild Curry Powder (storebought or homemade, see page 12)

1 1/4–1 3/4 cups Curry Masala Sauce (see page 22)

2 teaspoons tomato purée

1 teaspoon salt

Akhni Stock (see page 23) or water

4 fresh (or strained canned) tomatoes

2 teaspoons Garam Masala (storebought or homemade, see page 35)

1 tablespoon dry fenugreek leaves

1 tablespoon ground almonds

1 tablespoon fresh or bottled lemon juice

METHOD

■ Heat the ghee, and stir-fry the garlic for 1 minute.

■ Make a water paste of the turmeric, cumin, black pepper, and red pepper. Add to the garlic and fry for 1 minute. Add the onion and curry paste and fry for 2 minutes.

■ Add the curry masala sauce, using less if you want a dry curry and more for a liquid sauce. Stir-fry for a couple of minutes, then add the tomato purée and salt.

■ To obtain the correct consistency, either add akhni stock or water to taste. (You may need to add a little oil as well to keep the correct texture.) Add the tomatoes and the remaining ingredients.

■ Add your principal ingredient—1 1/2 pounds meat, chicken, seafood, or vegetables for 4 people—and when hot, serve.

Vindaloo Base

SERVES 4

The true vindaloo comes from Goa, a tiny coastal state in south-western India. This version is very hot and contains a little vinegar (*vin*) and potato (*aloo*). To make *bindaloo* or *tindaloo*, add more ground red pepper (or liquid hot pepper sauce).

INGREDIENTS

2 tablespoons ghee or vegetable oil

1 teaspoon Garlic Purée (see page 16)

1/2 teaspoon turmeric

1 teaspoon ground black pepper

2–4 teaspoons ground red pepper (cayenne)

1/2 Spanish onion, peeled and thinly sliced

1 tablespoon Curry Paste (storebought or homemade, see page 20) or Mild Curry Powder (storebought or homemade, see page 12)

1 1/2–1 3/4 cups Curry Masala Sauce (see page 22)

2 teaspoons tomato purée

1 teaspoon salt

Akhni Stock (see page 23) or water

6–8 (2-inch) pieces potato, boiled

2 teaspoons Garam Masala (storebought or homemade, see page 35)

1 tablespoon dry fenugreek leaves

1 tablespoon vinegar

METHOD

■ Heat the ghee, and stir-fry the garlic for 1 minute.

■ Make a water paste of the turmeric, black pepper and red pepper. Add to the garlic and fry for 1 minute. Add the onion and curry paste and fry for 2 minutes.

■ Add the masala sauce, using less if you want a dry curry and more for a liquid sauce. Stir-fry for a couple of minutes, then add the tomato purée and salt.

■ To obtain the correct consistency, either add akhni stock or water to taste. (You may need to add a little oil as well to keep the correct texture.) Add the potatoes and the remaining ingredients. Simmer for 5 minutes.

■ Add your principal ingredient—1 1/2 pounds meat, chicken, seafood, or vegetables for 4 people—and when hot, serve.

Phal Base

SERVES 4

Pronounced *pal* or *pol* and sometimes called Bangalore *phal*, this is the hottest curry found in Indian restaurants. There is nothing like it in India—it is pure invention. That's not to say they don't have hot curries in India, as the hottest curry I have ever had was in the southernmost part of India. It was a hot pepper curry and it used, I was told, six varieties of hot peppers including large mild green ones and tiny fierce red ones. The recipe apparently said "take 30 chillies per person…"

INGREDIENTS

2 tablespoons ghee or vegetable oil	1 1/2–1 3/4 cups Curry Masala Sauce (see page 22)
1 teaspoon Garlic Purée (see page 16)	2 teaspoons tomato purée
2 teaspoons ground black pepper	1 teaspoon salt
4 teaspoons ground red pepper (cayenne)	Akhni Stock (see page 23) or water
1 tablespoon Curry Paste (storebought or homemade, see page 20) or Mild Curry Powder (storebought or homemade, see page 22)	1 tablespoon chopped hot pepper pickle from a bottle
	Any hot pepper sauce to taste (optional)

METHOD

■ Heat the ghee, and stir-fry the garlic for 1 minute.

■ Make a water paste of the black pepper and red pepper. Add the garlic and fry for 1 minute. Add the curry paste and fry for another minute.

■ Add the curry masala sauce, using less if you want a dry curry and more for a liquid sauce. Stir-fry for a couple of minutes, then add the tomato purée and salt.

■ To obtain the correct consistency, either add akhni stock or water to taste. (You may need to add a little oil as well to keep the correct texture.) Add the remaining ingredients. Simmer for 5 minutes.

■ Serve after 5 or more minutes of simmering, or when ready.

■ Add your principal ingredient—1 1/2 pounds meat, chicken, seafood, or vegetables for 4 people—and when hot, serve.

Tandoori Cooking

The tandoor oven is made of clay, cylindrical in shape and wider at the base than at the top. It has no bottom and a hole at the top. The clay is fashioned by hand. It is allowed to dry and is not fired. It is merely put into place, often on or in the ground in the open air. Sizes vary: the biggest I've seen was about 4 feet high and the smallest 1 1/2 feet. Quite where this type of oven was invented is lost to history: it may have been India, or it may have been the Middle East, where one encounters similar clay ovens called *tandir* or *tonir*. Most restaurants have not one but two tandoors, one charcoal-fired running at temperatures of up to 700°F—the other gas-powered, operating at lower temperatures.

The flavor of tandoori food is outstanding and unique, the result of a combination of the marinade and the very high temperature of the charcoal. However, grilling on an ordinary barbecue will give almost the same flavors. Oven baking or grilling is the way most of us at home will cook our tandooris and tikkas, and recipes in this book are written for these methods.

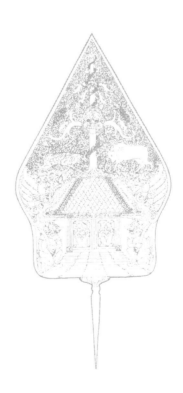

Tandoori Dry Mix Masala

YIELDS 10 (4-PERSON RECIPE)

If you intend to make a lot of tandoori dishes, it will be worth your while making up a batch of this spice masala. A dish for four requires a couple of tablespoons. This batch will fit in a large jar and be enough for about 40 individual portions (or 10 dishes for four). As with all pre-mixed masalas, it has the advantage of maturing during storage. Keep it in the dark in an airtight container, and it will be good for about 12 months.

INGREDIENTS

3 1/2 tablespoons ground coriander	5 teaspoons dried mint
3 1/2 tablespoons ground cumin	5 teaspoons beet powder (deep red coloring)*
3 1/2 tablespoons garlic powder	4 teaspoons ground red pepper (cayenne)
3 1/2 tablespoons paprika	1 teaspoon annatto seed powder (yellow coloring)*
5 teaspoons ground ginger	
5 teaspoons mango powder	

METHOD

- Simply mix the ingredients together well, and store.

- To use, follow the tandoori/tikka recipes.

*If you use food coloring powder instead, use only 1 teaspoon red and 1/2 teaspoon sunset yellow. These small quantities will achieve a more vibrant color than beet and annatto.

Tandoori Paste

Most restaurants use bright red tandoori paste to color and spice their marinade. It is not difficult to make your own. To cook, use one recipe of the previous tandoori dry masala and cook it following the method for curry paste on page 20.

Tandoori or Tikka Marinade

YIELDS
ENOUGH FOR
1 1/2 POUNDS
MEAT

Yogurt is used as the medium in which to suspend the spices for tandoori or tikka marinade.

INGREDIENTS

3/4 cup plain yogurt	3 tablespoons chopped fresh cilantro leaves
3 tablespoons mustard or canola oil	1 teaspoon roasted cumin seeds, ground
2 tablespoons bottled or fresh lemon juice	1 teaspoon Garam Masala (storebought or homemade, see page 35)
1 teaspoon Garlic Purée (see page 16)	1 tablespoon Curry Paste (storebought or homemade, see page 20)
1 teaspoon Ginger Purée (see page 16)	
3 fresh green hot peppers, chopped	2 tablespoons Tandoori Paste (see above) or Tandoori Dry Mix Masala (see page 30)
1 tablespoon chopped fresh mint or 1 teaspoon dried	1 teaspoon salt

■ Mix all ingredients together and use as called for to marinate and coat meat and fish dishes.

■ Recipes using this marinade include Tandoori Sardines, Lamb and Chicken Tikka Masala, Tandoori Trout, Goan Duck, and Aloo Makhanwala. (See index for page numbers.)

Miscellaneous

The following recipes don't strictly fall into any of the previous categories, so are headed as above—they're anything but miscellaneous in curry cooking though!

Ghee

YIELDS ABOUT
3 CUPS

Ghee is a clarified butter, which is very easy to make and gives and distinctive and delicious taste. When cooled and set, it will keep for several months without refrigeration.

If you want to make vegetable ghee, simply use margarine instead of butter.

INGREDIENTS

2 pounds butter

METHOD

■ Place the butter in a medium nonstick pan. Melt at a very low heat.

■ When completely melted, raise the heat very slightly. Ensure it does not smoke or burn, but don't stir. Let cook for about 1 hour. The impurities will sink to the bottom and float on the top. Carefully skim off the floating impurities with a slotted spoon, but don't touch the bottom.

■ Turn off the heat and allow the ghee to cool a little. Then strain it through paper towels or muslin into an airtight storage jar. When it cools, it solidifies, although it is quite soft. It should be a bright pale lemon color and it smells like toffee. If it has burned it will be darker and smell different. Providing it is not too burned, it can still be used.

Paneer Cheese

YIELDS ABOUT 8 OUNCES

This is a fresh homemade cheese that does not melt when cooked. It is full of protein and easy to make. It resembles cottage cheese and is very common in the subcontinent as a vegetarian dish.

INGREDIENTS

4–6 tablespoons any vinegar or lemon juice

9 cups whole milk

METHOD

■ Choose a large pan. If you have one of 2-gallon capacity, the milk will only occupy a third of the pan and won't boil over (unless the lid is on).

■ Bring the milk slowly to a boil. Add the vinegar or lemon juice, stirring until it curdles (when the curds separate from the whey).

■ Strain into a clean kitchen towel placed on a strainer over a saucepan. Fold the towel over and press the excess liquid—the whey—through. Keep for later use as stock.

■ Now place the curds—from now on called paneer—onto a draining board still in the towel. Press it out to a circle about 1/2-inch thick. Place a flat weight (the original saucepan full of water for instance) on the towel, and allow it to compress the paneer.

■ If you want crumbly paneer (as for page 120), remove the weight after 30–45 minutes. Crumble the paneer and use as the recipe directs.

■ If you want the paneer to be solid, keep the weight on for 1 1/2–2 hours. Then cut the paneer into cubes.

■ Cubed paneer is normally deep-fried to a pale golden color for best texture.

Tamarind Purée

Tamarind—also known as the Indian date—is a major souring agent, particularly in southern Indian cooking. The tamarind tree bears pods of about 6–8 inches long that become dark brown when ripe. These pods contain seeds and pulp, which are preserved indefinitely for use in cooking by being compressed into a rectangular block weighing about 11 ounces.

To use the tamarind block, soak it overnight in twice its volume of hot water—about 3 cups per 11-ounce block. The next day mash it well with your fingers, then strain through a sieve, discarding the husks. The brown liquid should be quite thick, and there will be plenty of it. Freeze any extra.

Garam Masala

YIELDS ABOUT
5 CUPS

Garam means hot and *masala* means mixture of spices, and there are as many combinations and recipes of garam masala as there are cooks who make it. Some use only five or six spices and I have one recipe that lists as many as fifteen spices! This one has only nine and has been my favorite for years. Try it. For the next batch, you might like to vary the mixture to your own preference. That's the fun of Indian cooking.

For an aromatic garam masala, use this recipe without the peppercorns and ginger.

(I came across a remarkably mild garam masala recipe in Kashmir which uses no hot spices at all. In their place were saffron stamens and rose petals. If you wish to use saffron, add it whole at the very end of cooking.)

INGREDIENTS

2 1/4 cups coriander seeds	1/2 cup brown cardamoms
2 cups cumin seeds	4 whole nutmegs
1/3 cup black peppercorns	1 cup bay leaves
1/2 cup cassia bark	3 tablespoons ground ginger
1/2 cup cloves	

METHOD

■ Lightly roast everything except the ground ginger under a low- to medium-heat broiler, or in an oven at about 325°F. Do not let the spices burn. They should give off a light steam.

■ When they give off an aroma—in the oven, 10 minutes is enough—remove from the heat, cool, and grind. A coffee grinder will do if you use small quantities and break up large items first.

■ After grinding, add the ground ginger, mix thoroughly and store in an airtight jar. Garam masala will last almost indefinitely, but it is always better to make small fresh batches every few months to get the best flavors.

Char Masala

YIELDS
ENOUGH FOR
4 CURRIES

Char in India, Urdu, and Afghan means four, and *masala*, our familiar mixture of spices. This is to Afghan cooking what garam masala is to Indian. Use it in the Afghan recipes in this book, or as a substitute for garam masala if you wish to have a very fragrant mixture of spices with no heat.

The four spices are usually the same, though the proportions can vary. This very fragrant recipe makes enough for four curries.

INGREDIENTS

1/4 cup cassia bark	2 tablespoons green cardamom *seeds* (not pods)
1/2 cup white cumin seeds	2 1/2 tablespoons cloves

METHOD

- Roast the spices under a low- to medium- heat broiler, or in an oven at 325°.

- When they give off an aroma, remove from the heat, cool, and grind.

- Store in an airtight jar.

Panch Phoran

This is a Bengali mixture of five (*panch*) spices. There are several possible combinations. This is my favorite. Use it in vegetable cooking, for example *Niramish* on page 119.

INGREDIENTS

White cumin seeds	Mustard seeds
Fennel seeds	Wild onion seeds
Fenugreek seeds	

METHOD

- Mix together equal parts of all ingredients.

STARTERS

▲▲▲▲▲▲▲▲▲▲▲▲▲▲▲▲▲▲

A meal of several courses is a Western concept born in an age gone by and brought to its height in Victorian times when course would follow course, and tables and diners would groan from the sheer weight of so much food.

In many parts of traditional India, the convention of courses is unknown. The complete meal is served at once—soups (thin curries), masalas (thick curries), rissoles and pastries, breads, rice and lentils, and sweets appear together each in a strictly predetermined place. Most of the people of village India adhere to this tradition. The minority city-dwelling middle class (some eighty million, nonetheless) have adopted Western conventions and are content to eat in two or three courses, but it is the Parsee community who cap everything with up to twenty courses at their formal dinners.

Kudhi

GUJERATI SOUP

SERVES 4

The first contact the English made with India was in 1608 when a Captain Hawkins, a sailor in the employ of King James I, landed in the northwestern state of Gujerat. Whether Hawkins tried the food of this mainly vegetarian state is not on record, but if he had he would certainly have tasted *kudhi*. It is a soup traditionally but optionally containing whey and chickpea-flour dumplings in its tasty sour-and-spicy yogurt base.

Kudhi, also called *kari,* is one of the possible derivatives of the word "curry" given to the world by the English.

INGREDIENTS

2 tablespoons ghee or vegetable oil	
1 cup plain yogurt	
2 tablespoons chickpea flour (*besan*)	
1 teaspoon Ginger Purée (see page 16)	
1–4 green hot peppers, chopped	
1/2 teaspoon salt	
1 1/4 cups water or Akhni Stock (see page 23) (or paneer whey, see page 33)	
2 teaspoons brown sugar	

SPICES

1 teaspoon mustard seeds
1/2 teaspoon fenugreek seeds
6 dry curry leaves
Pinch of asafoetida

METHOD

■ Heat the ghee or oil and fry all the **Spices** for 2 minutes in a saucepan large enough for the whole job.

■ Mix the yogurt and chickpea flour, then add the remaining ingredients. Stir in well. Place everything into the saucepan.

■ Simmer for 20 minutes, stirring from time to time.

■ Serve hot as a soup on its own or as a thin curry gravy with rice.

Mohinga

SPICY NOODLE FISH SOUP

SERVES 4

Burmese food is quite distinctive and unique, and sadly little known. It has evolved into a combination of Indian (robust and hot spicing), Chinese (noodles, bean sprouts, stir-frying), and Thai (fragrance and fish sauces). If one recipe is to be singled out to typify Burma it must be *mo-hi-nga*—literally noodle-spicy-fish soup. Indeed, it is referred to as the national dish. In Burma you buy *mohinga* from roadside stalls or from vendors who backpack their cooking apparatus and ingredients from house to house. It is a spicy, tart, fishy soup with a fascinating string of garnishes. The Burmese eat it as a complete main meal, but it also makes an ideal starter. The ingredients list looks a little formidable, but it is much simpler to make than it looks.

INGREDIENTS

2 tablespoons canola or sesame oil

2 teaspoons Garlic Purée (see page 16)

8 tablespoons Onion Purée (see page 17)

1 teaspoon *nga-pi* (shrimp paste)

1–6 (to taste) fresh green hot peppers, chopped

3 tablespoons chickpea flour (*besan*)

3 tablespoons flaked coconut, ground to a powder

1 (7-ounce) can sardines or herrings, boned

1 (8-ounce) can bamboo shoots

Akhni Stock (see page 23) or water

Juice of 2 lemons

Salt to taste

4 ounces egg noodles or vermicelli

GARNISHES

Hard-boiled egg slices

Chopped scallion

Chopped fresh cilantro leaves

Watercress or mustard and cress

Tiny prawn *pakoras* (lentil flour fritters)

Julienne of bell peppers (red, green, or yellow)

METHOD

■ Heat the oil, and fry the garlic for 1 minute, then add the onion and fry for 3 minutes. Add the *nga-pi* and mash and fry for 2 minutes, followed by the hot peppers for 2 minutes.

■ Mix the chickpea flour and coconut powder with enough water to make a thick paste. Add to the pan and stir over heat until it will thicken no more.

■ Transfer to a saucepan. Break the fish up, and add it and juices. Add chopped bamboo shoots and the liquid from the can.

■ Add enough akhni stock or water to bring it to consommé consistency, then add the lemon juice and salt to taste.

■ Cook the noodles in a separate pan according to the package directions. Drain.

■ To serve, place the noodles in a soup bowl and ladle the piping hot soup over them. Serve, allowing the diners to put their own choice of garnishes on the soup.

Ashak

PASTRY FILLED WITH LEEK, SPICY MEAT, AND YOGURT

MAKES
8 TO 10
SMALL
DUMPLINGS

Afghanistan has had the misfortune of being a passageway between Persia and the subcontinent. In fact, apart from sea routes, the passes through Afghanistan were the only way to reach India. Not surprisingly, Afghan food includes Iranian and Indian influences with such dishes as *biriani* and curries, but it also has a distinctive style of its own. *Ashak* is a lovely Afghan specialty. It consists of crescent-shaped stuffed pastries, boiled dumpling style, and served in a spicy sauce. The filling traditionally consists of Chinese chives or *gandana*, a type of long grass not unlike our leeks. *Gandana* is very occasionally available here but you can substitute leeks, ordinary chives, and/or scallions.

INGREDIENTS

DOUGH

4 cups white flour

1 tablespoon vegetable oil

1 egg

1/4 cup water

FILLING

3 cups chopped leek leaves, or scallions, chives, or a combination

1 garlic clove

2 tablespoons chopped fresh cilantro

1/2 teaspoon salt

1/2 teaspoon ground black pepper

SAUCE

3 tablespoons vegetable oil

1 teaspoon Garlic Purée (see page 16)

4 tablespoons Onion Purée (see page 17)

6 ounces ground lamb or beef, or tempe for vegetarians

1 tablespoon Char Masala (see page 36)

6 fresh tomatoes

1 tablespoon tomato purée

Salt to taste

GARNISHES

Plain yogurt or sour cream

Chopped fresh cilantro

- To make the dough, mix the flour with the oil, egg, and a little water—enough to create a smooth pliable dough. Let it rest for at least 1 hour.

- Meanwhile, make the filling. Grind the leaves, garlic, cilantro, salt, and pepper either in a mortar or in a food processor. Do not make it into a purée—rather just pulse it a few times, then put it into a strainer to drain.

- Start making the sauce about half an hour before you want to serve the *ashaks*. Heat the oil, and fry the garlic for 1 minute, then add the onion and fry for 3 minutes. Add the ground meat and the char masala spices. Stir-fry for another 10 minutes, then add the tomatoes and tomato purée. Simmer until ready to serve—for a minimum of 10 minutes—then add salt to taste.

- Knead the dough well, and roll out very thin, to about 1/16 inch for light *ashaks* (the thicker the pastry, the chewier the ashaks will be). Cut into 4-inch circles using a saucer or cutter. Re-roll spare pastry as necessary, trying to get 8 circles. (I got 10 the last time, with very thin pastry.)

- Place 1 tablespoon of the filling on half of the circle, then fold it over, tweaking the edges to seal it well. Shape it to the traditional crescent shape. Do the same with the remainder of the circles.

- Place them at once into a pan of simmering water. Carefully remove after 10 minutes.

- Place at once in a serving bowl, top with the hot sauce, then garnish with the yogurt or sour cream and fresh cilantro.

Aloo-Achar

COLD POTATO PICKLE

SERVES 4

Aloo or *alu* means potato and *achar* is pickle. This cold dish, spiced with pickle and yogurt, is sour and tangy in taste. It hails from the Himalayan-mountain country of Nepal, from whence come those hardy *sherpahs* (who enable Everest expeditions to succeed) and *ghurkas* (the fierce fighting troops so highly prized in the British army). Two other tough individuals live here—the mysterious yeti and the shaggy yak, beast of burden and milk and meat supply. In the bitterly cold winters, the Nepalese rely on their supply of dried foods and pickles. This dish is typical.

INGREDIENTS

1 pound potatoes, boiled	2 tablespoons Onion Purée (see page 17)
2 tablespoons mustard or canola oil	2 tablespoons fresh cilantro
1 teaspoon black mustard seed	2 teaspoons dried mint
2 teaspoons white sesame seed	2 tablespoons Curry Paste (storebought or homemade, see page 20)
1 teaspoon white poppy seed	
1 teaspoon Garlic Purée (see page 16)	2 tablespoons brinjal pickle, chopped up
1-2 teaspoons water	Salt to taste

METHOD

- Cool and dice the potato into 1/2-inch cubes.

- Heat the oil. Stir-fry the seeds (1 minute), the garlic purée (another minute), and the onion purée (2 more minutes).

- Add a little water to ease any sticking, then add in the remaining ingredients, including the diced potato. Stir well and remove from the heat. It should be dry. Serve cold.

Aloo Tama

POTATO COOKED WITH BAMBOO SHOOTS

SERVES 4

This is another Nepalese dish.

INGREDIENTS

12 ounces new potatoes	2 tablespoons chopped fresh cilantro
2 tablespoons vegetable oil	1/4 cup light cream
1 teaspoon Garlic Purée (see page 16)	Salt to taste
1 teaspoon Ginger Purée (see page 16)	SPICES
4 tablespoons Onion Purée (see page 17)	3 cloves
4 ounces bamboo shoots, canned or fresh	1-inch piece cassia bark
Water for simmering	1 teaspoon white cumin seeds
1–4 fresh hot peppers, chopped (to taste)	1 teaspoon paprika

METHOD

■ Scrub the potatoes and boil until nearly done. Drain and let cool.

■ While the potatoes are cooling, heat the oil and fry the **Spices** for 1 minute, the puréed garlic for 1 minute, the ginger purée for 2 minutes, and the onion purée for 3 minutes.

■ Dice the potatoes and bamboo shoots and add them to the pan with enough water, and no more, to allow them to simmer. Add the hot peppers, cilantro, and cream. Simmer for enough time to finish the cooking of the potato. Add salt to taste.

Chana Chat

CHICKPEA CURRY

SERVES 4
AS A STARTER

Chat pronounced "chart" and sometimes spelled "chaat" means snack or appetizer in Hindi, and this chickpea dish is particularly good cold served with crispy pappadoms or deep-fried puri bread. It is also nice hot.

INGREDIENTS

1 1/4 cups dried chickpeas	1 teaspoon dried fenugreek leaves
2 tablespoons vegetable oil	1 tablespoon Curry Paste (storebought or homemade, see page 20)
1 teaspoon white cumin seeds	
2 teaspoons white sesame seeds	1 tablespoon Tandoori Paste (see page 31)
1 teaspoon white poppy seeds	2 fresh tomatoes, chopped
1 teaspoon Garlic Purée (see page 16)	1 tablespoon tomato purée
2 tablespoons Onion Purée (see page 17)	2/3 cup tomato soup (canned)
2 tablespoons fresh cilantro	Salt to taste
1 teaspoon dried mint	

METHOD

■ Check that the chickpeas are free of grit, then rinse them and soak them in twice their volume of water for 6–24 hours.

■ Strain the chickpeas, rinse with cold water, then boil them in ample water for 40–45 minutes, until tender.

■ About 5 minutes before the chickpeas are ready, heat the vegetable oil. Stir-fry the seeds (1 minute), then add the garlic purée and cook for another minute, and then add the onion purée and fry for 2 more minutes. Add all the remaining ingredients. Stir fry for about 5 minutes.

■ Strain the chickpeas and add them to the sauce. Remove from heat and serve hot or allow to cool.

Sheek Kebab

GROUND BEEF COOKED ON SKEWERS

MAKES 4 LARGE OR 8 SMALLER KEBABS

Kebabs are said to have originated in Turkey, indeed, the word means "cooked meat" in Turkish. *Shish* means skewer and this has become *sis*, *sheesh*, or *sheek* as the method migrated eastwards into India. Mutton would have been the traditional meat, pounded on the grinding stone with the roots and spices. Many tandoori restaurants use beef. Use a food processor to achieve a moldable, glutinous texture. The kebab mixture is also used for the filling *keema naan* (page 147).

INGREDIENTS

1 1/2 pound flank steak, top round, or tenderloin steak (the better the meat the better the kebab)

4–6 garlic cloves, chopped

1-inch piece fresh ginger, chopped

2–4 green hot peppers, chopped (to taste)

2 tablespoons chopped fresh cilantro leaves

1 teaspoon garlic powder

1 teaspoon dried mint

2 tablespoons Curry Paste (storebought or homemade, see page 20)

1 teaspoon Tandoori Paste (see page 31)

METHOD

■ Inspect the meat. Remove fat, skin, and gristle if any. Chop it coarsely.

■ Mix the meat well with all the other ingredients, then process or mince it to a fine texture.

■ Mix it all again, using the fingers—it's messy, but the fingers are a chef's best tools! Divide into four (or eight).

■ Using metal skewers, shape each portion of meat on the skewer into a long sausage of about 6 inches. The smaller kebabs should be about 3 inches in length.

■ Preheat the oven to 375°F, place the kebabs on an oven tray, and bake for 15 minutes. Or use a broiler at about three-quarters heat, rotating the kebabs a few times.

■ Serve on a bed of lettuce with a lemon wedge and chutneys.

Rashmi Kebab

KEBAB IN AN EGG NET

**SERVES 4
AS A STARTER**

This is a finely ground lamb or beef kebab wrapped inside a netlike omelet casing. The net casing itself requires a little practice and patience, and an altogether much simpler method is to make a very thin omelet and wrap the kebab inside. The net appears in many Oriental dishes from Afghanistan to Thailand. It is interesting to attempt and once mastered you have a dish that looks professional and unusual.

INGREDIENTS

1 recipe Sheek Kebab (see page 45)	NET
Vegetable oil for deep-frying	2 large eggs, beaten

METHOD

- Divide the kebab mixture into four.

- Shape into small flat circles (flying saucers) and cook as for sheek kebabs in the previous recipe.

- To make the egg net, heat plenty of oil in a deep frying pan to 325°F. Test with a flick of egg, which should float sizzling, but not burn. Then drip the egg off the fingers, slowly moving across the pan to form a grid. Use about half an egg per grid. Lift the grid out as soon as it is formed and wrap it around the cooked kebab. Repeat three more times.

Nargissi Kofta Ke Bahar

INDIAN "SCOTCH EGG"

**SERVES 4
AS A STARTER**

Scotch egg is the best way to visualize this dish. The traditional meat is ground lamb, but as with the previous kebab recipe, beef is acceptable, wrapped around a hard-boiled chicken egg.

I have developed a very interesting variation for this dish. Instead of red meat, I use chicken breast wrapped around a hard-boiled chicken or duck egg. My favorite variation uses quail eggs (note the short boiling time) for really dainty *koftas*—serve two per person.

INGREDIENTS

	SPICES
8 quail (or 4 chicken or duck) eggs	1/2 teaspoon cumin
10 ounces chicken breast, skinned and boned	1/2 teaspoon coriander
1-inch cube fresh ginger	1/2 teaspoon paprika
2 garlic cloves	1/2 teaspoon Garam Masala (storebought or homemade, see page 35)
2–4 fresh hot peppers (optional, to taste)	
1 tablespoon chopped fresh cilantro leaves	2 teaspoons dry fenugreek leaves
4 tablespoons semolina	1 teaspoon Curry Paste (storebought or homemade, see page 20)
Vegetable oil	

METHOD

■ Hard boil the quail eggs for about 4 minutes in boiling water (15 minutes for chicken or duck eggs), then run under cold water. To prevent them from cracking, ensure they are at room temperature and prick the blunt end with a pin before boiling.

■ Chop the chicken breast and ginger, garlic, and hot peppers and place all this with the **Spices** and fresh cilantro in a food processor. Make this mixture into a coarse purée by pulsing.

■ Divide the mixture into eight (or four) and wrap it around the shelled eggs, achieving a round or egg shape. Roll the shapes in the semolina and place on an oven tray. Glaze with oil.

■ Preheat the oven to 375° F. When hot, put the tray in and bake for 15 minutes. Serve hot.

Shashlik Kebabs

SERVES 4

Shashlik literally means "meat and vegetables on a skewer." The word comes from the Russian (Armenian) "to grill." The shashlik method no doubt traveled from the Middle East, through Iran (where the same style of cooking is called the *hasina kebab*) and eventually into India. As far as the method goes, it is straightforward, and has probably been around as long as cooking itself. What could be easier than to pick up a piece of meat on the tip of a sword and grill it over fire? Here I use bamboo skewers.

Served on a bed of lettuce, topped with mustard and cress, parsley, cilantro, and a lemon or lime wedge, it not only looks great but is healthy, being low in calories and high in proteins and vitamins, especially if you eat the garnish salad.

INGREDIENTS

16 (1-inch) cubes skinned chicken breast, or 16 similarly sized pieces lamb (*or a combination*)

1/2 each of red pepper, green pepper, and yellow pepper, seeded

1 Spanish onion, peeled

4 lemon or lime wedges

4 green hot peppers (optional)

MARINADE

6 tablespoons mustard or canola oil

1 teaspoon garlic powder

1 tablespoon dried mint

1 tablespoon Curry Paste (storebought or homemade, see page 20)

1/2 tablespoon salt

METHOD

■ Immerse the diced chicken or lamb in the marinade for 24 hours.

■ Strain off the surplus marinade. If barbecuing, place the meat or chicken on metal skewers and heat over charcoal for 10–15 minutes for chicken, 20–25 minutes for lamb. If broiling, place the meat or chicken on foil on the broiler pan located on the middle rack under moderate heat. Cook for the same times, turning once or twice. With either method, baste occasionally with marinade.

■ During the cooking, cut the three peppers into 1-inch diamond shapes, and the onion the same.

■ Once the meat or chicken is cooked, transfer it to four bamboo skewers (if hot, use tongs), interspersed with the peppers, onions, lemon wedge, and hot pepper. Finish off over charcoal or under a broiler until sizzling and fully hot. Serve at once.

Bengali Fish Kebabs

SERVES 4

Bengal is a Hindu State in the northeast of India. It shares its border, and India's most sacred river, the Ganges, with Bangladesh (formerly East Bengal), now an independent Muslim state. It was religion that divided Bengal in 1947, but the culinary tradition of both Bengals remains identical, and the fish from the Ganges and Hougli rivers and the Bay of Bengal are prolific and important.

INGREDIENTS

1 pound cod steaks	2/3 cup plain yogurt
1 teaspoon Garlic Purée (see page 16)	Salt to taste
1 teaspoon Ginger Purée (see page 16)	1 teaspoon turmeric
2 tablespoons Onion Purée (see page 17)	2 teaspoons Garam Masala (storebought or homemade, see page 35)
1–4 hot peppers, chopped (to taste)	Ghee for basting

METHOD

- Cut the fish into 1-inch cubes. Wash, drain, and dry them.

- Mix all the remaining ingredients, except for the ghee, to form a marinade paste. Marinate the cubes in this for 2 hours or so.

- Thread the fish onto four bamboo skewers, and broil as in the previous shashlik recipe for 10 minutes. Then baste with ghee and serve on a bed of salad.

Maachli Qutabshai

DRY SPICY FRIED FISH

SERVES 4

This dish, its name from *maachi* (fish) and *qutabshai* (dedicated to a twelfth-century Afghan-Turkish conqueror who raised the status of Delhi from provincial town to fortress capital), gives a whole new insight into fish cooked in batter. But you can, of course, use shellfish, chicken, other white meat, or vegetables.

INGREDIENTS

8 fish fillets (use sole or another white-fleshed fish)	1 teaspoon white cumin seeds
	1 teaspoon caraway seeds
4 tablespoons vinegar	4 tablespoons chopped fresh cilantro leaves
Juice of 2 lemons	
Salt to taste	1–4 green hot peppers, chopped (to taste)
BATTER	
1 1/4 cups chickpea flour (*besan*)	3 eggs
1 1/4 cups white flour	Salt to taste
1 teaspoon Garlic Purée (see page 16)	Vegetable oil, for deep-frying

METHOD

■ Wash the fish fillets and marinate in the vinegar, lemon juice, and salt for 30 minutes.

■ Drain the fish, reserving the marinade. Make the batter by simply mixing all the batter ingredients together with the reserved marinade. By using no water, it will be crisper.

■ Dip the fish in the batter and half fry, until it starts to crisp. Remove from the oil, set aside for a few minutes, then fry again until golden brown.

Shrimp Pathia and Puri

SERVES 4

*P*athia is a dry-fried sweet-and-sour dish from Bombay's Parsee community. It goes beautifully with shrimp. *Puri* are the small brown flour bread disks which, when deep-fried, puff up like little balloons. The shrimp *pathia* is simply stir-fried and place on the *puri*, garnished with fresh cilantro, and served piping hot.

INGREDIENTS

1 pound tiny shelled, deveined shrimp (you want them as small as possible)	1 tablespoon flaked coconut, ground to a powder
4 tablespoons ghee or vegetable oil	2 teaspoons prawn *ballachung* (prawn pickle)
2 teaspoons Garlic Purée (see page 16)	1 1/2 tablespoons brown sugar
6 tablespoons Onion Purée (see page 17)	Salt to taste
2 tablespoons Curry Paste (storebought or homemade, see page 20)	*Puris* (see page 149)
1 tablespoon tomato purée	GARNISH
	Chopped fresh cilantro leaves

METHOD

■ Prepare and wash the shrimp. Drain and set aside.

■ Heat the ghee or oil, and fry the purées and pastes for 5 minutes, then add the shrimp, coconut, pickle, sugar, and salt to taste.

■ Simmer for 10 minutes, adding enough water to prevent sticking.

■ Make the *puris* as on page 149.

■ Serve on the *puris*, and garnish with some cilantro.

Shrimp Butterflies

SERVES 4

By fanning the shrimp's tail before dipping in the batter, the butterfly appearance is achieved.

INGREDIENTS

4 jumbo shrimp, around 4 ounces each

BATTER (instructions on page 50)

1 1/4 cups chickpea flour (*besan*)

1 1/4 cups white flour

1 teaspoon Garlic Purée (see page 16)

1 teaspoon white cumin seeds

1 teaspoon caraway seeds

4 tablespoons chopped fresh cilantro leaves

1–4 green hot peppers, chopped (to taste)

3 eggs

Salt to taste

Vegetable oil, for deep-frying

METHOD

■ Carefully shell and devein the shrimp, but keep the tail shells on them. Fan out the tails and flatten them with a cleaver.

■ Immerse the shrimp entirely into the batter and deep-fry at 375°F for about 10 minutes.

■ Serve at once on a bed of salad, otherwise the batter becomes soggy and chewy.

MEAT

▲▲▲▲▲▲▲▲▲▲▲▲▲▲▲▲▲▲

Contrary to popular belief, meat eating is quite widespread in India, especially among certain groups. Most of the Indian population is Hindu, to whom the cow is sacred. Those who do eat meat enjoy mutton and goat; they would have no aversion to eating pork, but rarely get the opportunity to do so. Hindus do not eat beef or veal.

The worship of the cow pre-dates the establishment of the Hindu religion. In fact, it goes back to the nomadic cattle-breeding tribes of Aryans, who entered India around 1500 BC, displacing the literate and very civilized Harrapan incumbents of the Indus valley. The Aryans originated in the Caucasus, and branches spread west as far as the Danube and east as far as China, and across the Levant to Iran (to whom they bequeathed the country's name) and on through into north India. With them went their herds of cattle. These they raised and used not only for dairy products, but for leather and for meat. As the tribes grew and diversified, their descendants gradually changed the emphasis more to dairy farming and less to meat. This may well have been because of the shortages of livestock. Eventually the Hindu religion emerged; the cow became venerated and was no longer eaten.

The Islamic laws relating to food are very similar to those of Judaism. Jews must only eat food that is kosher (fit and proper), while to Muslims it must be *halal* (clean). To fail to eat thus would be unthinkable to true practitioners of both religions. Kosher and *halal* food must be prepared and eaten according to unbreakable rules. Meat must be slaughtered, then butchered in a particular way, and blood must not be present in the meat ready for cooking.

Common to both religions is a proscription on the eating of pork. The animal is considered to be unclean, its flesh the carrier of disease, and a strict orthodox Jew or Muslim would be unable to contemplate its consumption. The origins of this are obscure. Uncleanliness and disease are not satisfactory reasons—pork has been the primary meat of the Far East for millennia—and the true answer may lie in the fact that pigs, being rooters, simply did not thrive in desert conditions. The few that did, apart from being scarce, may well have been diseased. Jews are not permitted to eat rabbit, shellfish, or any meat cooked or served with dairy products, but these rules do not apply to Muslims. The Iranians, on the other hand, developed a style of cooking in which meat is marinated in yogurt, undoubtedly originating from the time of the Aryans. It is a technique widely used in the northern curry lands to this day.

The most popular meats eaten by Muslims are mutton or goat (lamb being a luxury for special occasions), and chicken. Beef is permitted and enjoyed, although cattle in the form of cows, oxen, or buffalo are uncommon. Horse meat is as unlikely to be eaten on the subcontinent as it is in the United States although the Mongols from whom the Moghul emperors were descended undoubtedly ate horse. The Moghuls almost certainly did not.

The pig could thrive in many parts of India but few are to be seen except in Goa. Goans are Christian Indians and they adore pork. Pork has always been the number one meat in Burma, Thailand, Indo-China, and China. The Chinese, by the way, eat beef as well, but rarely mutton. They detest all dairy products, especially milk which they regard as an offensive-smelling liquid about as appetizing as saliva. But then they eat dog and locusts . . . it's a strange world.

Sultani Pasanda

BEATEN SLICED MEAT CURRY

SERVES 4

*P*asanda means "beaten." Traditionally, mutton would be used, but beef gives much better results, as we are able to get such excellent quality beef. Veal, lamb, even duck breast, can be used with equal success in this superb recipe.

INGREDIENTS

1 1/2 pound lean lamb or beef steak in one piece	8 tablespoons Onion Purée (see page 17)
6 tablespoons ghee or vegetable oil	1 tablespoon Garam Masala (storebought or homemade, see page 35)
2 teaspoons Garlic Purée (see page 16)	1 teaspoon ground mace
2 teaspoons Ginger Purée (see page 16)	2/3 cup light cream
10 green cardamom pods, seeds extracted	2 tablespoons ground almonds
1 cup milk	1 tablespoon white sugar
	Salt to taste

METHOD

■ Ask the butcher for lamb steak. It is a fatless top of leg piece which can be beaten. If this is unavailable, use good quality beef steak. Slice the meat into four, then beat it to about 1/4 inch thick. Halve each so that you have 8 pieces.

■ Heat the ghee or oil and stir-fry the garlic purée for 1 minute and then the ginger purée for 1 minute.

■ Add the cardamom seeds to the pan with the meat. Stir-fry to sear for 2 minutes per side. Add half the milk, and lower the heat to simmer.

■ After 10 minutes or so, add the onion purée, the garam masala, and mace. Stir-fry until it starts simmering, then add the remaining milk. Continue simmering, stirring occasionally, for another 10 minutes. What you are aiming to do is to soften the meat by gentle simmering in liquid—not *boiling*—so you must not allow the liquid to reduce too much, nor must there be too much. By the end of this stage, the meat should begin to be tender and it should not be dry.

■ Add the cream, almonds, and sugar, and simmer until the meat is completely tender. Keep the liquid balance correct. Add salt to taste.

55

Achar Gosht

MEAT COOKED IN PICKLE

SERVES 4

I first came across this recipe in Nepal where the severe winters call for resourceful methods of drying meat and vegetables and producing fantastic pickles in the brief but hot summer. With readily available supplies of meat (*gosht*) in the West, this recipe uses tender cuts of lamb, beef, or pork simmered with *brinjal* (eggplant) pickle, chutney, and, if available, fresh mango slices to give a curry with a rich, sweet, sour, and savory taste.

INGREDIENTS

1 1/2 pound lean lamb, cubed	Akhni Stock (see page 23) or water
4 tablespoons ghee or vegetable oil	1 fresh mango, cut into strips
1 recipe portion Curry Masala Sauce (see page 22)	2 tablespoons chopped fresh cilantro leaves
2 tablespoons Curry Paste (storebought or homemade, see page 20)	Salt to taste
4 tablespoons *brinjal* (eggplant) pickle, chopped	

METHOD

■ Trim the meat of any fat, gristle, etc., and preheat the oven to 375°F.

■ Heat the oil in a casserole, and stir-fry the curry masala sauce for 3 minutes, then the paste for 3 minutes. Add the *brinjal* pickle and the meat. Mix well, then place in the preheated oven.

■ After 20 minutes, inspect, stir, and taste. Add akhni stock or water if required. Return to the oven.

■ After 20 minutes, check again. This time add the fresh mango (if available), cilantro, and salt to taste. Turn off the heat but leave the casserole in the oven to reach ultimate tenderness and absorb the flavors.

Note: Alternatively, stir-fry on top of the stove for 45 minutes or until tender.

Rhogan Josh Gosht

AROMATIC LAMB

SERVES 4

Another Moghul dish using whole aromatic spices, it is very fragrant when cooked in the correct traditional manner. Many curry houses simply make a standard medium-hot curry to which they add bell peppers, onion, and tomato. *Rhogan* is sometimes referred to as a Kashmiri dish. No doubt the emperors partook of it there, and wherever they happened to be, but its true origin appears to be Iran. *Rhogan josh*, I am reliably informed, means "boiled in ghee" in Persian. It is dark in color and traditionally this was exaggerated to a dark red by use of *ratin jot* (alkanet root) which, when fried, gives the ghee a deep beet color, leading to one interpretation that it means cooked in red juices.

In the Kashmiri language it means red meat and the *wazas*, the feast cooks, use a purplish red flower called cockscomb, which grows in the spring, is dried and powdered, and sprinkled into the cooking. In this recipe I have used beet powder to achieve the effect of the cockscomb.

This recipe is a traditional Kashmiri recipe, using no garlic, ginger, onion, or spurious vegetables; it does not have a long marinating time; yogurt is used to create a sauce; and the method brings out the fragrance of the spices.

INGREDIENTS

6 tablespoons ghee or vegetable oil	6 cloves
1 1/2 pound lean lamb, cubed	1 teaspoon fennel seeds
2/3 cup plain yogurt	SPICES 2 (GROUND)
Akhni Stock (see page 23) or water	1 tablespoon Garam Masala (storebought or homemade, see page 35)
1 tablespoon fresh cilantro leaves	
Salt to taste	1 tablespoon beet powder (optional)
SPICES 1 (WHOLE)	1/2 teaspoon asafoetida
2 brown cardamoms	1/2–2 teaspoons ground red pepper (cayenne)
6 green or white cardamoms	
4-inch piece cassia bark	1 tablespoon ground white poppy seeds
4 bay leaves	1 teaspoon ground cassia or cinnamon

METHOD

■ Heat the oil in a casserole and fry **Spices 1** for 1 minute. Add the meat and sear it, stir-frying for 5 minutes. Add the yogurt, mix in well, and place in a preheated oven at 375°F.

■ Inspect, stir, and taste after 20 minutes. Add a little akhni stock or water if it needs it.

■ Inspect, stir, and taste after another 20 minutes. This time put in **Spices 2**, the fresh cilantro, and salt to taste. Return to the oven. Turn off the heat, but leave the casserole in the oven to allow the meat to become completely tender and absorb all the flavors.

■ Spoon off all excess oil (keep for future use) before serving.

Note: Alternatively stir-fry on stove for 45 minutes or until tender.

Podina Gosht

LAMB COOKED WITH MINT

SERVES 4

Another aromatic dish, with the mint giving a remarkable sweetness and lightness.

Follow the recipe for *Methi Gosht* (pages 63–64), but use either:

INGREDIENTS

3 tablespoons dried mint or 6 tablespoons
    fresh spearmint (or a combination),
    stems removed and leaves chopped in
    place of the fenugreek

Lamb Korma

LAMB IN MILD CREAMY SAUCE

SERVES 4

The *korma* was created for the Moghuls. It was said that if a chef could cook a *korma* he could cook for the court. If he could cook two dozen variations he would be "king of the kitchens," and cook only for the Emperor's table. One cook, it is said, had a repertoire of 365 *kormas*—one for every day of the year. Be that as it may, the Emperor's personal cook held a position of enormous power and influence at court. One can picture the extraordinary dishes that must have issued forth from those royal kitchens. Indeed, at the deserted city of Fatehphur Sikri near Jaipur, the kitchen building stands perfectly preserved. It was simply abandoned with the rest of Emperor Akbar's great new walled city when the water supply ran dry in 1600, just fourteen years after it was built.

With its gentle use of fragrant and aromatic whole spices and its garlic, ginger, and creamy sauce, *korma* is perfect for the person who claims to dislike curry. No one could possibly fail to fall in love with it.

But a *korma* must be cooked in the traditional manner. This excellent recipe is most certainly fit for the table of an emperor. It is finished off with *tarka*—a fried mixture.

INGREDIENTS

1 1/2 pound fatless, boned lamb, cubed

2/3 cup ghee or vegetable oil

2 tablespoons Garlic Purée (see page 16)

1 tablespoon Ginger Purée (see page 16)

8 tablespoons Onion Purée (see page 17)

2 teaspoons sugar

1 teaspoon salt

1 cup plain yogurt

3/4 cup light cream

Akhni Stock (see page 23) or water

SPICES 1 (WHOLE)

6-inch cinnamon stick

12 green cardamoms

10 cloves

8 bay leaves

1 teaspoon fennel seeds

SPICES 2 (GROUND)

1 teaspoon cumin

2 teaspoons coriander

2 teaspoons coriander

2 teaspoons Mild Curry Powder (store-bought or homemade, see page 12)

TARKA (ADDITIONAL SPICING)

3 tablespoons ghee

1/3 teaspoon fenugreek seeds

1/2 teaspoon cumin seeds

3 tablespoons finely chopped onion

GARNISH

2 teaspoons sliced almonds

METHOD

- Trim the meat of any gristle, etc., and preheat the oven to 375°F.

- Heat the ghee or oil, then fry **Spices 1** for 1 minute, add the garlic purée and fry for 1 minute, the ginger purée for 1 minute, and the onion purée for 3 minutes. Add the sugar and salt.

- While this is frying, make a paste of **Spices 2** and a little water, then stir-fry it into the purée mixture for a final couple of minutes.

- Combine the spice mixture with the lamb, place in a casserole, and cook in the oven for 25 minutes.

- Remove, inspect, and stir, then mix in the yogurt and cream. Return to the oven for 20 more minutes.

- Meanwhile, cook the *tarka* (the additional spicing). Heat the ghee and stir-fry the seeds for 1 minute. Add the onion and fry until golden brown.

- Remove the casserole from the oven, inspect, then stir in the *tarka* and, if necessary, a commonsense amount of akhni stock or water if it looks too dry. Taste for tenderness. Judge how much more baking you need to reach complete tenderness. It will probably need at least 10 minutes more. It can be served immediately, garnished with the sliced almonds, or reheated next day (some people prefer that, saying it is more marinated), or it can also be frozen.

Note: Alternatively, stir-fry on top of the stove for 45 minutes, or until tender.

Jardaloo Sali Boti

LAMB COOKED WITH APRICOT

SERVES 4

The Parsee community fled from Iran (Persia) about 1,100 years ago to escape religious persecution. They settled eventually in Bombay, when it was nothing more than lagoons and swamps, having first been given sanctuary in Gujarat state. Parsee food is as unique as the people themselves. Its origins are unmistakably Persian, with delightful combinations of meat, nuts, and dry fruit.

The names of two of their dishes—*dhansak*, lamb cooked in a purée of lentils and vegetables, and *patia*, seafood in a sweet-and-sour hot sauce—are part and parcel of the standard curry house menu, but it is rare to find an establishment which cooks them with true Parsee lightness of touch. The lamb with its creamy sweet-and-sour sauce is enhanced by the apricot and nuts, and the crisp potato matchsticks (*sali*) set the dish off to perfection and are well worth the effort to make.

INGREDIENTS

1 1/2 pound lean lamb or other meat, cubed

1/3 cup any vinegar

6 tablespoons ghee or vegetable oil

2 teaspoons Garlic Purée (see page 16)

2 teaspoons Ginger Purée (see page 16)

1 Spanish onion, peeled and thinly sliced

3 tablespoons ground almonds

3 tablespoons mixed whole nuts (pistachio, hazel, and almond)

1 tablespoon brown sugar

1 tablespoon tomato purée

6–8 dried apricots, sliced

Akhni Stock (see page 23) or water

1 tablespoon chopped fresh cilantro leaves

Salt to taste

SPICES 1 (WHOLE)

3 teaspoons cumin seeds

6–8 brown cardamoms

1 teaspoon cloves

4-inch piece cassia bark or cinnamon stick

SPICES 2 (GROUND)

2 teaspoons cumin

2 teaspoons coriander

1 teaspoon cassia or ground cinnamon

1/2 teaspoon green cardamom

1/2 teaspoon black pepper

1/2 teaspoon ground fennel seeds

METHOD

■ Trim the meat of any fat, gristle, etc., and preheat the oven to 375°F.

■ Place the meat, vinegar, and **Spices 1** into a lidded casserole, and put in the preheated oven for 20 minutes.

■ Meanwhile, heat the oil, and stir-fry the garlic purée for 1 minute, then the ginger purée for 1 minute, **Spices 2** for 1 minute, and the onion for 5 minutes.

■ When the casserole comes out of the oven, add all the remaining ingredients except for the cilantro and salt. Stir, add a little water or akhni stock if it needs it, and return the casserole to the oven.

■ After another 20 minutes, take it out again. Inspect, stir, taste. Add the fresh cilantro and salt to taste.

■ Return to the oven, which can now be turned off. Serve when the meat is tender. Garnish with *sali* (page 64).

Note: Alternatively, stir-fry on top of the stove for 45 minutes—or until tender.

Methi Gosht

MEAT WITH FENUGREEK LEAF

SERVES 4

*M*ethi, pronounced "maytee," is fenugreek, which comes in three forms—seeds, fresh leaves, and dried leaves. (*Gosht*, of course, means mutton, lamb, or goat.) This dish comes from the Punjab, an area now part in Pakistan and part in the north of India. Punjabi cooking is very spicy and colorful. Dishes such as *keema, kofta, sag gosht, paratha, halva,* and the legendary *tandoori* originated in the Punjab. Moghul dishes such as *korma, pasanda, rhoghan gosht, pullaos,* and *biriani* are also in the Punjabi repertoire, because the great Moghul city of Lahore was, until 1947, in the Punjab. The savory, rich, creamy-textured spicy curries of the Punjab are very much to the taste of Western curry addicts.

This dish is one of the most savory. I find that dried *methi* leaf is more concentrated and easier to get than the fresh leaf, which can become very bitter and black in color if cooked too long.

INGREDIENTS

1 1/2 pound lean lamb or stewing beef, cubed	Akhni Stock (see page 23) or water
4 tablespoons ghee or vegetable oil	4 tablespoons dried fenugreek leaf, ground, or 6 tablespoons fresh fenugreek leaves, destalked and chopped (or a combination)
1 recipe portion Curry Masala Sauce (see page 22)	
2 tablespoons Curry Paste (storebought or homemade, see page 20)	Salt to taste

METHOD

■ Trim the meat of any fat, gristle, etc., and preheat the oven to 375°F.

■ Heat the oil in a casserole, and stir-fry the curry masala sauce for 3 minutes, then the paste for 3 more minutes. Stir in the meat, and place in the oven.

■ After 20 minutes, inspect, stir, and taste. Add akhni stock or water, if required. Replace in the oven.

■ Meanwhile, if using fresh *methi*, boil some water, blanch the leaves for 1 minute, then strain.

■ After another 20 minutes, inspect, stir, and taste the casserole contents. The meat should be tender by now. Add a little more water if needed, also the fenugreek and salt. Replace the casserole, turning off the oven heat. It should be ready after 10 minutes, but it can stay in the oven until you are ready to serve.

Note: Alternatively, stir-fry on top of the stove for 45 minutes—or until tender.

A Selection of Starters: *Shashlik Kebabs* (page 48), *Nargissi Kofta* (page 47), *Shrimp Butterflies* (page 52).

Counter-clockwise: *Lamb Korma* (page 59), *Medium Curry* (page 25), *Chicken Tikka Masala* (page 93), *Madras Curry* (page 26).

Four Unusual Curries: *Pili-Pili Chicken* (page 92), *Rhogan Josh Gosht* (page 57), *Sri Lankan Duck* (page 101), *Machher Jhol* (page 106).

Some Exotic Dishes: *Stuffed Baked Glazed Quail* (page 97), *Noor Mahal Biriani* (page 144), *Anarkali Bahar/Sizzling Tandoori Chicken* (page 95).

Top: (counter-clockwise) *Quick Lemon Rice* (page 137), *Jardaloo Sali Boti* (page 61), *Cachumber Punjabi* (page 154), *Coconut Chutney* (page 155), *Paneer Cheese* (page 33). Center: *Puri* (page 149), Bottom: *Bundghobi Poriyal* (page 123), *Lobster Korma* (page 111), *Plain Boiled Rice* (page 135).

Some Vegetable Delights: *Niramish* (page 119), *Sag Wala* (page 117), *Chana Chat* (page 44), *Bombay Potato* (page 128).

Accompaniments: *Pullao Rice* (page 140), *Tarka Chana Dhal* (page 133), *Naan Bread* (page 146) (with various chutneys and accompaniments).

The Sweet Trolley: *Kesari Shrikhand* (page 162), *Coconut Pancakes* (page 161), *Moira Banana* (page 165).

Lamb Tikka Masala

LAMB IN TANDOORI SAUCE

SERVES 4

Halfway between Delhi and Kashmir, 7,000 feet up in the foothills of the Western Himalayas, lies Simla. It was created by the British in the 1830s and become their summer capital—a place to which they could retreat from the intense heat in the plains, in the same way that the Moghuls escaped the sun at Kashmir. Eventually several hill stations were built. They have in common a cool summer climate, hairpin roads to reach them, wonderful rose-filled gardens surrounding detached bungalows, churches, and sporting clubs. Simla was the setting for Rudyard Kipling's *Plain Tales from the Hills*. It was so British—and to this day it is a cool summer playground for wealthy Indians.

The food eaten by the Brits of the Raj was more likely to be roast mutton and potatoes than lamb *tikka masala*, but this recipe has become a favorite.

INGREDIENTS

1 1/2 pounds lean lamb, cubed	3 tablespoons Curry Masala Sauce (see page 22)
1 cup Tandoori Marinade (see page 31)	1 teaspoon white sugar
SAUCE	Juice of 1 lemon
3 tablespoons ghee or vegetable oil	
4 ounces ground beef or lamb	

METHOD

■ Trim the mutton well and marinate it in the tandoori marinade for a minimum of 6 hours and a maximum of 30 hours.

■ Preheat the oven to 375°F. Place the meat with the marinade on an oven tray and cook for 20 minutes. Baste and taste. Continue until tender (another 20 minutes at least).

■ Meanwhile, heat the ghee or oil, and fry the ground meat and curry masala sauce for 20 minutes, adding water as needed to keep it from sticking. Add the sugar and lemon juice and continue to stir-fry. Add more curry masala sauce to achieve the texture of your choice.

■ Add the cooked, cubed meat and its liquid to the curry mixture. Simmer to blend, and then serve.

Lamb Palak

LAMB COOKED WITH SPINACH

SERVES 4

Picture, if you will, a balmy evening just after the sun has set. On a lake in Udaipur a marble Maharaja's palace appears to be floating on the water in the purple-red dusk.

I will always remember that scene, how we approached the palace, now the Lake Place Hotel, by launch. My appetite was whetted by the knowledge that the royal chefs of the ex-prince of Udaipur were laying a special banquet to be served on palace-silver *thalis*. It was pure fairyland—and the dinner was equally magical. It was not a complicated meal—the main course consisted of just one meat dish, mutton *palak*, accompanied by plain rice, breads, and chutneys—but it was divine, a meal to remember.

A variation of mutton *palak* is *sag gosht*, popular at many Indian restaurants.

INGREDIENTS

1 pound lean lamb, cubed	1/3 cup light cream
1 tablespoon Garam Masala (storebought or homemade, see page 35)	Salt to taste
1/3 cup plain yogurt	**SPICES**
12 ounces fresh spinach, washed and chopped	1 teaspoon turmeric
	1 teaspoon garlic powder
6 tablespoons ghee or vegetable oil	1 teaspoon ground red pepper (cayenne)
6 teaspoons Garlic Purée (see page 16)	1 teaspoon whole cumin seeds
8 tablespoons Curry Masala Sauce (see page 22)	2 teaspoons Mild Curry Powder (storebought or homemade, see page 12)
Akhni Stock (see page 23) or water	

METHOD

- Marinate the lamb with the garam masala and yogurt for 24 hours or so.

- Blanch the spinach in boiling water, then purée it.

- Heat the oil and stir-fry the **Spices** for 2 minutes, then the garlic purée for 2 minutes. Add the curry masala sauce and the spinach purée, and stir-fry until simmering.

- Place all the ingredients into a lidded casserole and put into a preheated oven at 375°F.

- Inspect, stir, and taste after 20 minutes. Add a little water or akhni stock if needed. Continue cooking.

- Stir and taste after 20 more minutes. Add cream and salt. Serve when absolutely tender.

Zafrani Kofta

SPICED MEATBALLS WITH SAFFRON

SERVES 4

Kofta curries are yet another of the favorite Moghul dishes. *Koftas* (ground spicy meatballs) are easy to mold but retaining the ball shape during cooking is not always easy, as they tend to break up. I have slightly modified this recipe, therefore, to give you a foolproof method of cooking the balls by using your oven (a piece of equipment not at hand at the time of the Moghuls and still a rare sight in Indian villages).

The creamy sauce colored with saffron, combined with the aromatically spiced balls, is pure Moghul and is a dish rarely encountered in restaurants. I collected this recipe in Agra, and it is one of the specialties of a Kashmiri kebab chef who works at Agra's extraordinarily elegant Moghul Sheraton Hotel. He can neither read nor write. He simply learned his trade from his father who was a chef, as did his father's father, and so on right back to the court of Emperor Shah Jahan. In the 1600s, the capital of the empire was Agra, and Shah Jahan undertook much building, including the Taj Mahal, built as a tomb for his wife. To do all this work it was necessary to bring in skilled labor from all parts of the empire, and the town just outside the Taj is still populated by the descendants of those laborers. Favorite chefs would certainly be required, too, so I see no reason to doubt that, twelve generations or so ago, one of Shah Jahan's chefs was preparing *zafrani kofta* in Agra. Why should his descendant not be preparing the identical dish handed down a mere twelve times in today's Indian palace—the luxury hotel?

INGREDIENTS

MEATBALLS

1 1/2 pound lamb leg steak, or beef

1 teaspoon Garlic Purée (see page 16)

1 teaspoon finely chopped fresh cilantro leaves

1/2 teaspoon salt

MEATBALL SPICES (GROUND)

4 brown cardamoms

4 green cardamoms

1 teaspoon ground cassia or cinnamon

1/2 teaspoon salt

SAUCE

1/3 cup vegetable oil

2 teaspoons Garlic Purée (see page 16)

2 teaspoons Ginger Purée (see page 16)

8 tablespoons Onion Purée (see page 17)

2/3 cup plain yogurt

2/3 cup whipping cream

2 tablespoons tomato purée

20 strands saffron

Salt to taste

SAUCE SPICES (GROUND)

2 teaspoons coriander

1/2 teaspoon turmeric

1/2 teaspoon ground red pepper (cayenne)

METHOD

■ Trim excess fat off the meat, then dice it and grind—ideally in a food process (in India it would be hand beaten).

■ Add the garlic purée, cilantro, salt, and the **meatball spices**. Mix well with your hands, then divide into 12 equal balls.

■ Place them on an oven tray, then bake in an oven preheated to 325°F for 20 minutes.

■ During this, begin making the sauce. Heat the oil and fry the garlic purée for 1 minute, the ginger purée for 2 minutes, and the onion purée for 3 minutes. Add the **sauce spices** and stir-fry for 2 minutes.

■ Now fold in the yogurt and cream, tomato purée, and saffron. Stir-fry until simmering.

■ Just before adding the cooked meatballs, check that there is enough liquid in the sauce. You will probably need to add some (use the liquid from the oven tray if any and/or water to get a nice texture). Add the balls and some salt. Simmer until hot, then serve.

Raan

SPICY-COATED ROAST LEG OF LAMB

SERVES 4

Leg of lamb suits the tandoori process, and this recipe is one of the culinary gems from Moghul India. As with all tandoori cooking, the secret lies in marinating for at least 24 hours (48 is even better for this particular dish). The spicing is especially aromatic in this recipe.

INGREDIENTS

3 1/2–4-pound leg of lamb on the bone

MARINADE

2/3 cup plain yogurt

2 teaspoons Garlic Purée (see page 16)

2 teaspoons Ginger Purée (see page 16)

2 tablespoons ground almonds

2 teaspoons flaked coconut, ground to a powder

1 teaspoon salt

1/3 cup vegetable oil

SPICES

1 tablespoon Tandoori Paste (see page 31)

1 tablespoon Garam Masala (storebought or homemade, see page 35)

1/2 teaspoon ground green cardamoms

1/2 teaspoon ground fennel seeds

2 teaspoons poppy seeds

2 teaspoons dried mint

GARNISHES (OPTIONAL)

20–30 whole almonds, roasted or fried

2 tablespoons chopped fresh cilantro leaves

METHOD

■ Stab the lamb all over to the bone with a sharp knife to enable the marinate to penetrate the meat.

■ In a bowl large enough to hold the meat, mix all the remaining ingredients—the marinade and the **Spices**—into a paste.

■ Put the meat into the bowl of paste, and poke the paste into all the gashes, ensuring the meat is well coated.

■ Leave in the refrigerator to marinate for a minimum of 24 hours, a maximum of 48. The longer you leave it, the better the paste will seep in and adhere to the meat during cooking.

■ Preheat the oven to 350°F, and slow-roast the lamb for about 3 hours. When really tender, the flesh should literally fall off the bone. Prior to serving, let it rest for 30 minutes or so in a low oven.

■ An optional garnish is to press roasted or fried whole almonds into the gashes, then sprinkle with fresh cilantro.

Balti Gosht

POT-ROASTED MEAT

SERVES 4

Galti is an Urdu word, and refers to a special bucket-shaped pot used for cooking in the central part of Pakistan, around Lahore. It is a traditional winter-time preparation when village families get together around a charcoal fire and cook *balti gosht* in the *balti* hanging over the charcoal fire. It is usually eaten with *naan* bread. In Pakistan they drink *sherbat* with it.

INGREDIENTS

1 1/2 pound leg of lamb, cubed, *or* 2 1/4 pounds lamb on the bone	2 fresh tomatoes, quartered
1 1/2 cups water	1 teaspoon cumin seeds, roasted
4 garlic cloves, chopped	1 tablespoon chopped fresh cilantro leaves
1 teaspoon salt	
4 tablespoons vegetable oil	SPICES
1 Spanish onion, peeled and chopped	4-inch piece cassia bark or cinnamon stick
1/2 red bell pepper, diced	6 whole cloves
1–4 fresh hot peppers, chopped (to taste)	6 brown cardamoms

METHOD

■ Wash the lamb, then place it in a lidded casserole or saucepan with about 1 1/2 cups water. Add the garlic, salt, and **Spices**.

■ Either place in a preheated oven at 375°F or on the stove, and cook, covered, until just tender (about 45 minutes). Inspect from time to time, then remove from heat, and let it stand in its steam with the lid still on, for 20 minutes or so.

▪ Meanwhile, heat the oil in a large *karahi*, fry the onion until golden, then add the red pepper, hot peppers, and tomatoes. Cook until it is nearly dry (about 10 minutes on a low heat).

▪ Then add the drained meat to the *karahi*, with a little of the liquid. Stir-fry until it becomes quite dry, adding the cumin seeds and the fresh cilantro about 5 minutes before it is ready.

▪ The dish is served in cast-iron *karahis* (also called *baltis* in the Lahore area). You can serve it any way you wish, but serving the correct way does seem to enhance it.

Kurzi or Kashi

FESTIVE WHOLE LAMB

**SERVES
16 TO 20**

The walls of Shah Jahan's magnificent Lal Qila Red Fort in Delhi are 100 feet high and enclose an area of 124 acres. Built into the wall are six huge arched gates, large enough to admit processional elephants. The most important entrance was the Kurzi, or Khirzi, gate which led directly from the fort's river frontage to the Emperor's private apartments. It was the gate through which Shah Jahan entered to inaugurate the building in 1648 and through which all important dignitaries entered the fort to attend the Emperor. Above the Kurzi gate is an overhanging balcony contained within a domed octagonal tower at which the ruling emperor would appear each sunrise before large waiting crowds.

The most festive Indian dish is called the *kurzi*, or *kashi*. There is one restaurant in London where you can pay about $800 for a single dish. It is, in fact, a whole lamb baked in a mixture of spices, stuffed with basmati rice, and it serves at least twenty-five people.

The *kurzi* dish is usually a leg of lamb, about 3 1/2–4 pounds, which will serve four. Make up about one-third quantity of the marinade, and follow the recipe, adjusting baking times according to weight. It is prepared in advance to allow the marinade to seep in.

The smallest whole lamb you can get is between 8–12 pounds. You can get the whole carcass boned and rolled so that it will easily go into your oven, and will feed sixteen to twenty people. Alternatively you can ask for kid goat, starting at 10 pounds. Good butchers will oblige. It makes a great conversation piece at a dinner party—and, quite frankly, it's really easy to cook.

INGREDIENTS

1 whole baby lamb, 8–12 pounds

MARINADE

4 tablespoons Garlic Purée (see page 16)

6 tablespoons Ginger Purée (see page 16)

2 1/4 cups Onion Purée (see page 17)

2/3 cup plain yogurt

2/3 cup vegetable oil

2 teaspoons salt

SPICES

1 teaspoon ground red pepper (cayenne)

1 teaspoon turmeric

2 teaspoons ground coriander

2 teaspoons Mild Curry Powder (store-bought or homemade, see page 12)

1 teaspoon ground white cumin

1 tablespoon Garam Masala (storebought or homemade, see page 35)

6 bay leaves

8 brown cardamoms

10-inch piece cinnamon stick

1 teaspoon black cumin seeds

8 cloves

GARNISHES

Roasted almonds

Mustard and cress

Chopped fresh cilantro leaves

METHOD

■ Mix up the marinade ingredients, including the **Spices**, and let it stand for about an hour to blend well.

■ Wash the lamb and remove any surface fat. Prick it all over with the knife point quite deeply to assist the marinade to penetrate.

■ Preheat the oven to 350°F. While it is warming up, choose a good-sized baking tray and coat the lamb with the marinade. Reserve some marinade for later basting.

■ Roast the lamb for 1 hour, then remove and baste with more marinade. Return to the oven and continue for another whole hour. Baste again. Exactly how long the process will take depends on the weight of the lamb, but allow at least 30 minutes per pound and allow between 20–30 minutes for it to rest in a low oven before serving. But because of variations in oven temperatures or the tenderness of the meat, you *must* check how things are going by inserting a knife point into the lamb during cooking. So, with the slow-cooking method, a 10-pound lamb will take 5 hours to cook plus the resting time.

■ To serve, you must aim for maximum impact, so place the whole cooked lamb on a large oval serving platter. The meal can be served with a festive rice (Navrattan Pullao, for example), a tasty vegetable dish, and plenty of curry sauce. Garnish the lamb by placing it on a bed of rice and by liberally sprinkling it with roasted almonds, mustard and cress, and fresh cilantro.

Rempah

MALAY CURRY

SERVES 4

Malaya had for centuries been a rendezvous for spice traders from China, India, and Arabia before it became Muslim in 1414. The Portuguese brought Christianity and their ways to the area a century later and the Dutch and British followed. Singapore, at the tip of the thumb-shaped peninsula, was established in 1819 by Sir Stamford Raffles in the name of Britain.

All these cultural influences have left a remarkable melée of religions, languages, and culinary styles. Malaysian cuisine combines the best of Indian and Chinese with a sprinkling of Thai thrown in. Coconut, lemongrass, tamarind, five-spice powder, and curry spices combine to produce an aromatic, tangy, yet creamy curry. Adjust the cayenne quantity to your taste.

INGREDIENTS

1 large onion, peeled and roughly chopped	**SPICES (GROUND)**
6 garlic cloves	1 teaspoon coriander
1–6 fresh hot peppers (to taste)	1/2 teaspoon cumin
1 red bell pepper, seeded	1/2 teaspoon five-spice powder
2-inch cube fresh ginger	1/2 teaspoon garlic powder
6 tablespoons ghee or vegetable oil	1/4 teaspoon lemongrass powder
1 1/2 pound lean lamb or beef, cubed	1 teaspoon paprika
1/3 to 1/2 cup milk	1/4 teaspoon ground red pepper (cayenne)
1/2 cup coconut cream	1/2 teaspoon turmeric
3 tablespoons flaked coconut	1 teaspoon flaked coconut, ground to a powder
2 tablespoons Tamarind Purée (see page 34)	
Akhni Stock (see page 23) or water	

METHOD

■ Add enough water to the **Spices** to make a stiff paste, then let stand for a few minutes.

■ Make a purée of the onion, garlic, hot peppers, bell pepper, and ginger.

■ Heat the oil and fry the spice paste for 5 minutes or so; stir to prevent sticking. Then add the purée and fry for 15 minutes.

- Combine the cubed meat with the above in a casserole and place in an oven preheated to 375°F. Cook for about 1 hour.

- Meanwhile heat the milk with the coconut cream.

- Halfway through the cooking of the casserole, add the coconut cream, flaked coconut, and tamarind purée to the dish. Stir, and add water or stock if it needs it.

Keema Punjabi Masala

PUNJABI MINCED CURRY

SERVES 4

Ground meat is particularly good curried. *Keema* (mince) appears on the menus of a good many curry houses, but it is not the most popular dish, probably because it's one of those dishes most people don't bother to try. But try it you should: It is relatively inexpensive, it has a splendid texture, it cannot be overcooked—timings are not critical (so it makes a good dish for the beginner to try)—and it is very tasty.

INGREDIENTS

3/4 cup vegetable oil
4 teaspoons Garlic Purée (see page 16)
3 teaspoons Ginger Purée (see page 16)
3/4 cup Onion Purée (see page 17)
1-3 teaspoons water
2 tomatoes, chopped
2 tablespoons tomato purée
1 tablespoon flaked coconut, ground to a powder
1 1/2 pound lean ground lamb
Juice of 1 lemon

1 green bell pepper, seeded and chopped
Salt to taste

SPICES

2 teaspoons Garam Masala (storebought or homemade, see page 35)
2 tablespoons Mild Curry Powder or Curry Paste (storebought or homemade, see pages 12 and 20)
1 teaspoon poppy seeds
Up to 3 teaspoons ground red pepper (cayenne) (to taste)

METHOD

- Heat the oil and fry the garlic, ginger, and onion purées for, respectively, 1 minute, 2 minutes, and 5 minutes.

- Make a paste of the **Spices**, using a little water, then add and fry for 3 minutes.

- When bubbling, add the tomatoes, tomato purée, and coconut, then add the lamb.

- Place in a casserole and put into a preheated 375°F oven for 20 minutes, then check, stir, and add some water if necessary.

- Add the lemon juice, chopped pepper, and salt, and continue braising for another 20 minutes. Serve. (You could also stir-fry on the stove for the same amount of time.)

Magaz

BRAIN CURRY

SERVES 4

It was the British who created Pakistan in 1947. It was done with some reluctance and with the best of intentions, but it caused a lot of bad feelings among the Hindu and Muslim communities. Muslims were the majority in northwest and northeast India—the heartlands of former Arab, Turkish, Persian, and Moghul invaders—but measured over all India, they represented just 10 percent of the population. With the departure of the British Raj, the Muslims feared it would be replaced with a Hindu Raj that would persecute the Muslim minority. Partition came about in 1947, largely because of the efforts of one man, Mohammed Ali Jinna. This traditional tasty Punjabi dish originated in Pakistan.

INGREDIENTS

2 tablespoons any vinegar	**SPICES**
1 pound lamb's brain (2–3 brains, depending on the size of the lambs)	2 teaspoons Mild Curry Powder (store-bought or homemade, see page 12)
2 tablespoons vegetable oil	2 teaspoons Garam Masala (strorebought or homemade, see page 35)
6 tablespoons Curry Masala Sauce (see page 22)	1 teaspoon turmeric
1 tablespoon chopped fresh cilantro leaves	1/2 teaspoon ground red pepper (cayenne)
Salt	

METHOD

- Mix the **Spices** with the vinegar, and let stand for a while.

- Wash the brains, then cut into bite-sized pieces. Place the pieces in a bowl with the spice paste, and enough water to cover. Let stand for 1 hour.

- Heat the oil in a *karahi* or wok, and stir-fry the curry sauce for 5 minutes.

- Add the brains with the marinade and simmer until cooked—about 20 minutes—stirring occasionally.

- Add the cilantro and salt to taste. Simmer a few minutes more, then serve.

Puttan

KIDNEY CURRY

SERVES 4

INGREDIENTS

1 pound lamb's kidneys, trimmed, washed, and cut into bite-sized pieces	SPICES
2 teaspoons salt	1/2 teaspoon turmeric
1/3–1/2 cup any vinegar	1 teaspoon ground ginger
6 tablespoons ghee or vegetable oil	1 teaspoon ground red pepper (cayenne)
2 teaspoons Garlic Purée (see page 16)	2 teaspoons Mild Curry Powder (store-bought or homemade, see page 12)
8 tablespoons Onion Purée (see page 17)	
Akhni Stock (see page 23) or water	

METHOD

- Let the kidneys stand in a marinade of the salt and vinegar for about 1 hour.

- Mix the **Spices** with a little water to make a paste.

- Heat the ghee in a *karahi* or wok, and stir-fry the garlic purée for 1 minute, then the onion purée for 3 minutes. Add the spice paste and stir-fry for another 3 minutes.

- Add the kidneys and their marinade, and stir-fry to sear. Simmer for 20 minutes, adding stock or water as required.

West Indian Goat Curry

SERVES 4

The Spanish attempted to reach India by sailing due West. Christopher Columbus landed in the islands off America in 1492. He believed he had reached India, and the misnomer "West Indies" has remained. Centuries later, when the West Indies came under British rule, they settled numbers of Indians there, and with them came their cooking.

West Indian goat curry is a celebrated dish. Use goat, if you can get it, or mutton or lamb. The end result is slightly sweet, but omit the sugar if you prefer. To give the dish a really Caribbean flavor, add a shot of rum before serving.

INGREDIENTS

1 1/2 pound best-quality lamb, mutton, or goat

1 large onion, peeled and chopped

4 garlic cloves, chopped

2-inch piece fresh ginger, chopped

4 tablespoons vegetable oil

3/4 to 1 cup water

1 green bell pepper, seeded

4 tomatoes

4 slices fresh or canned pineapple

1 tablespoon brown sugar

Salt to taste

SPICES 1 (GROUND)

1 teaspoon turmeric

1 teaspoon coriander

1 teaspoon cumin

2 teaspoons paprika

SPICES 2 (WHOLE)

1/2 teaspoon coriander seeds

3 green cardamoms

1 teaspoon black peppercorns

2-inch piece cassia bark or cinnamon stick

METHOD

■ Cut the meat into 2-inch cubes discarding unwanted fat and gristle, etc. Wash it and let it dry.

■ Fry the onion, garlic, and ginger in the oil until golden.

■ Make a paste of **Spices 1** with a little water and add to the onions. Fry for another 10 minutes, stirring continuously. Add water to keep it from sticking.

■ In a casserole, combine the onion, **Spices 2**, the meat and 3/4 to 1 cup water. Cook in a preheated 375°F oven for 30 minutes.

■ Add the remaining ingredients and salt, stir well, and cook for another 10–15 minutes. Serve with brown rice and wedges of lemon.

Venison Curry

SERVES 4

Skkim is a tiny Buddhist state in the northeast of India, its neighbors being Nepal, Tibet, and Bhutan. Its original mountain people—called Lepchas—are good hunters, catching fish in the mountain streams and wild boar or wild deer, which are considered a Lepcha delicacy. Another of their favorite treats is the larvae of a particular wasp which they eat with chopsticks. I regret I do not have the recipe for this dish.

Herds of wild deer exist in certain parts of India, although they are not as prevalent as they are in Africa. Venison is now easier to come by from the city butchers of Delhi and Bombay—indeed, there are large venison farms near Bombay. It is a powerfully flavored meat, not to everyone's taste perhaps, but it curries well, although I would not try to be too subtle with spicing. Venison, by the way, was a great favorite with the Moghul emperors.

INGREDIENTS

1 1/2 pound best-quality venison, diced	1 teaspoon ground cumin
3 tablespoons ghee or vegetable oil	2 teaspoons paprika
1 tablespoon Garlic Purée (see page 16)	1 teaspoon turmeric
1 tablespoon Ginger Purée (see page 16)	**SPICES 2**
8 tablespoons Onion Purée (see page 17)	1 tablespoon Garam Masala (storebought or homemade, see page 35)
1 (15-ounce) can tomatoes	1 tablespoon dry fenugreek leaf
SPICES 1	
1 teaspoon ground red pepper (cayenne)	
2 teaspoons ground coriander	

METHOD

■ Wash excess blood off the meat and trim any unwanted pieces.

■ Heat the oil and stir-fry the garlic, ginger, and onion purées for 1 minute, 2 minutes, and 5 minutes respectively.

■ Meanwhile, open the can of tomatoes and strain, reserving the liquid. Mix the tomato juice from the can with **Spices 1** to get a runny paste, and preheat the oven to 375°F.

■ Add the paste to the purée mixture, stirring to prevent sticking, and fry until the water evaporates (about 5–8 minutes). When the oil floats to the top, it is done. Take off the heat and set aside.

■ In a casserole, heat the meat on the stove (at a medium-high heat) for 10–15 minutes to remove excess fluids. Strain, reserving liquid.

■ In the casserole, combine the purée-paste mixture, the meat, and the tomatoes. Put into the preheated oven and cook for 40 minutes. At the start it should neither be too dry nor too runny. Check from time to time, stirring, and add sufficient reserved meat liquid to keep it creamy and fluid, not dry.

■ After 40 minutes, add **Spices 2**, stir well, and continue cooking for 15 or so minutes. The meat should be cooked by now, but if it is still chewy, continue cooking until you are satisfied.

Sag Venison

Follow the above recipe but add twelve ounces spinach, either fresh—washed, chopped, and blanched—or canned. Add it to the meat with the purée-paste mixture and proceed with the recipe as above.

CHICKEN

▲▲▲▲▲▲▲▲▲▲▲▲▲▲▲▲▲▲

We are very lucky—complacent even—with the quality of chickens we get in the West. They are great plump, succulent birds yielding plenty of meat. On the subcontinent most of the birds are scrawny and tough, probably because they scratch out a rather less well-fed existence than their factory-bred cousins in the West. This is ironic because the chicken almost certainly originated in the jungles of India some fifty thousand years before people found their way there. In today's India, the chicken is a luxury item, although intensive farming is beginning to creep in around major cities.

Yet chicken is, in my view, the perfect meat for currying. It is quick to cook, tender, and delicious. Always remove and discard the skin.

Turkey is an excellent substitute for chicken in any of the following recipes. However, it is not part of the tradition of the curry lands.

Bangladesh Kurma or Korma

MILD CHICKEN CURRY

SERVES 4

This mild, most-aromatic dish makes an interesting comparison with the lamb *korma* recipe on page 59. Chicken breast is succulent and perfect with the aromatic spices, cream, yogurt, and nuts. The saffron strands give the dish a lovely pale yellow color. Do not use turmeric here: The color it gives is a little on the green side of yellow. This is a sumptuous dish, ideal for dinner parties or for first-time curry diners.

INGREDIENTS

1 teaspoon ground saffron powder or yellow food coloring	1/4 cup plain yogurt
4 tablespoons milk	2/3 cup whipping cream
6 tablespoons ghee or vegetable oil	2 tablespoons ground almonds
1 1/2 pounds chicken breast, skinned and cubed	20 saffron strands
	Salt to taste
4 teaspoons Garlic Purée (see page 16)	GARNISHES
8 teaspoons Onion Purée (see page 17)	2 tablespoons chopped fresh cilantro
2 teaspoons Garam Masala (storebought or homemade, see page 35)	30 whole almonds, roasted

METHOD

■ Mix the saffron powder or coloring with milk and set aside.

■ Heat the ghee or oil and quickly sear the chicken cubes by turning frequently for 2 minutes, then add the yellow milk and stir-fry for 2 minutes.

■ Add the garlic purée and stir-fry for 1 minute, then the onion purée for about 3 minutes—enough to remove the moisture content. Now add the garam masala and stir-fry for 2 more minutes. Your total frying time is around 10 minutes, and the chicken is half cooked.

■ Add the yogurt, cream, and ground almonds and when it starts to simmer, turn the heat down and stir-fry for 10 minutes more to ensure it does not stick, adding milk or water as necessary.

- Place the saffron strands in a little warm water and extract as much color as you can by gently mashing with a teaspoon.

- Check that the chicken is fully cooked by cutting through a large piece. Continue simmering if required. Just before serving, add the saffron and salt to taste. Garnish with the cilantro and almonds, and serve immediately.

Murgh Badam Pasanda

CHICKEN PASANDA WITH NUTS

SERVES 4

INGREDIENTS

4 chicken breasts, boned and skinned	**MARINADE**
3 tablespoons ghee or vegetable oil	2/3 cup plain yogurt
1/2 Spanish onion, peeled and chopped	1 teaspoon Ginger Purée (see page 16)
1 teaspoon Garlic Purée (see page 16)	2 teaspoons ground white pepper
1/3 cup cashew nuts	1 teaspoon ground cloves
1/2 teaspoon ground cloves	1 teaspoon ground coriander
1/4 teaspoon ground green cardamoms	1/2 teaspoon ground aniseed
1/2 teaspoon turmeric	**GARNISHES**
1 teaspoon ground white pepper	Toasted slivered almonds
1 to 1 1/4 cup water	Chopped fresh cilantro leaves or fresh parsley

METHOD

- Combine the marinade ingredients. Liberally brush the marinade on the chicken. Cover and refrigerate for several hours.

- Remove the chicken from the marinade and set the latter aside for later use.

- Sauté the chicken over medium heat in the ghee or oil until golden brown—about 3 or 4 minutes each side. Remove the chicken and set aside.

- Fry the onion, garlic purées, and cashews in the same pan until they are golden brown—about 2 minutes.

■ Take the pan off the heat and scrape the contents into a food processor or blender. Add the cloves, cardamom, turmeric, pepper, and 1/4 cup water to the blender or processor. Purée into a paste.

■ Return the paste to the frying pan and simmer over medium heat for 5 minutes, stirring occasionally. Add 3/4 to 1 cup water and the chicken with the reserved marinade, and continue to stir-fry for another 15–20 minutes.

■ Sprinkle with toasted almonds and the cilantro or parsley before serving. Accompany the dish with white rice and coconut chutney.

Murgh Masalam or Kurzi

WHOLE BAKED CHICKEN

SERVES 4

Kurzi chicken is served on special occasions (as is the lamb version on pages 72–73). Sometimes called *murgh masalam*, the dish requires a whole chicken which is marinated in a masala paste for up to 24 hours. It is then stuffed with a spicy ground meat and cooked.

I have in my recipe collection a book called *The Cooking Delights of the Maharajas*, written by the ex-Maharaja of the state of Sailana, and it includes recipes of his own and of other royal families in India. Two of the recipes are different ways of preparing this dish. One is skewer-cooked over charcoal or in the tandoor. The other method is intriguing, if a little impractical, but I feel sure you would like to know that the Maharaja recommends the stuffed chicken be placed in an earthenware pot at the bottom of which cinnamon sticks are spread crosswise in such a way that the chicken shall not touch the pot. Place the chicken in the pot and close with the lid. Prepare a thick paste of black beans, flour, and water. Seal the edges of the lid with the paste. Dig a round pit 18 inches deep and 18 inches wide in dry ground, light 20 cow-dung cakes and let them burn until white ash appears. Then put some in the pit. Put the pot in and put the remaining burning dung around and on top of it. Remove after 2 hours, and serve. I would dearly like to try this age-old authentic method!

Meanwhile, with sincere thanks to Maharaja Diguijaya Singh, here is a modified version of this fabulous dish. I have given quantities for four as usual, but it can easily be increased by using a larger chicken. For a really splendid occasion, use a turkey. A 10-pound turkey will serve twelve.

INGREDIENTS

1 roasting chicken, about 3 1/2 pounds

Ghee or vegetable oil for basting

MARINADE

1 teaspoon turmeric

2 tablespoons ground coriander

2 teaspoons Garam Masala (storebought
or homemade, see page 35)

2 teaspoons salt

8 tablespoons Onion Purée (see page 17)

4 tablespoons Curry Paste (storebought or
homemade, page 20)

FILLING

8 ounces Sheek Kebab meat mixture,
uncooked (see page 45)

2–4 whole potatoes, peeled

METHOD

■ Skin the chicken, wash, and dry it.

■ Make up the marinade and thoroughly coat the chicken. Marinate in the refrigerator for 6 hours.

■ When you want to cook the chicken, preheat the oven to 375°F.

■ Stuff the meat mixture into the chicken cavity, filling the remaining space with the whole raw potatoes.

■ Place the chicken on a rack on an oven tray and bake for 20 minutes per pound. Baste every 15 minutes with ghee. On the hour for a 3 1/2-pound bird, increase the heat to 425°F, and give it a final 10 minutes at that heat.

■ Reduce the oven temperature to low and allow the chicken to rest for about 15 minutes before serving.

Chicken Dhansak

CHICKEN COOKED WITH LENTILS AND VEGETABLES

SERVES 4

The authentic *dhansak* is a Parsee dish. Mutton is slowly cooked with lentils and vegetables, and it is one of the best-loved dishes, regarded as a special Sunday dinner. You can use meat, seafood, or vegetables for this recipe. Simply adjust timings up or down as needed. The Parsees would traditionally serve brown rice with *dhansak*.

INGREDIENTS

3/4 cup red lentils (*masoor dhal*)	Akhni Stock (see page 23) or water
3/4 cup water	1–2 pieces canned pineapple, drained and chopped
4 tablespoons vegetable oil	3–4 cups diced mixed vegetables (carrot, potato, peas, eggplant, beans, okra, tomato, bell pepper)
1 teaspoon turmeric	
8 tablespoons Curry Masala Sauce (see page 22)	
1 pound chicken breast, skinned and cubed	1 tablespoon sugar
	Salt to taste
2 tablespoons Curry Paste (storebought or homemade, page 20)	1 tablespoon Garam Masala (storebought or homemade, see page 35)

METHOD

■ Sift through the lentils and rinse them, then cook by boiling in 3/4 cup water. They will be cooked sufficiently in about 30 minutes.

■ Meanwhile, heat the oil in a *karahi*, stir-fry the turmeric for a few seconds, then add a spoonful of curry sauce. Take a quarter of the chicken and stir-fry it, searing it and coloring it yellow. Add more sauce, the next quarter of chicken and so on until all the sauce and chicken are used. Add the paste and a little stock or water.

■ Simmer for about 10 minutes, then check to see whether the chicken is cooked. When it is, combine with the remaining ingredients, and mix well. When simmering it is ready to serve.

Bhoona Chicken

DRY STIR-FRIED CHICKEN

SERVES 4

This is a simply dish to make using stir-fry techniques. The cooking takes 20 minutes, the preparation no more than 5—less time than it takes to heat up a frozen meal. Quickly prepare a rice dish and you have instant curry and rice.

INGREDIENTS

2 tablespoons ghee or vegetable oil	**SPICES 1 (WHOLE)**
1 1/2 pounds chicken breast, skinned and cubed	4 bay leaves
1 teaspoon turmeric	6 small pieces cassia bark or cinnamon stick
8 tablespoons Curry Masala Sauce (see page 22)	6 cloves
2 tablespoons chopped fresh cilantro leaves	**SPICES 2 (GROUND)**
	1 tablespoon Garam Masala (storebought or homemade, see page 35)
2 tablespoons plain yogurt	1–2 teaspoons ground red pepper (cayenne) (to taste)

METHOD

■ Heat the oil and fry **Spices 1** for 1 minute.

■ Add the chicken with the turmeric, and stir-fry for 5 minutes. Then add a spoonful of sauce, stir until it is absorbed, about 2 minutes, then add more. Repeat this process until the sauce is all used. The chicken should be fairly dry and nearly cooked after about 15 minutes.

■ Now add **Spices 2**, the fresh cilantro, and the yogurt. Stir-fry another 2–3 minutes and serve.

Chicken Jalfrezi

SERVES 4

This dish is colorful and incredibly simple to make, taking just 20 minutes. It not only tastes fresh but the chicken takes on a golden glow from the turmeric and it is highlighted by the greens and reds of the peppers.

INGREDIENTS

1 1/2 pounds chicken breast, boned and skinned	2 tablespoons chopped fresh cilantro leaves
4 tablespoons ghee or vegetable oil	2 or 3 fresh tomatoes, chopped
2 teaspoons white cumin seeds	Salt to taste
4 garlic cloves, finely chopped	Lemon juice
2-inch piece fresh ginger, finely chopped	SPICES
1 large Spanish onion, peeled and chopped	1 teaspoon paprika
2 green hot peppers (or more to taste), finely chopped	1/2 teaspoon turmeric
1/2 each of green and red bell peppers, seeded and coarsely chopped	2 teaspoons Mild Curry Powder (store-bought or homemade, see page 12)

METHOD

■ Cut the chicken into bite-sized pieces.

■ Heat the oil and fry the cumin seeds for 1 minute. Add the garlic and fry for 1 minute, then add the ginger and fry for another minute.

■ Add the chicken pieces and stir-fry for about 10 minutes. The chicken should look white and nearly cooked. Lift the chicken out with a slotted spoon and set aside.

■ Heat the remaining juices on the stove, and when hot, fry the **Spices** for 3 minutes. Add the onion and hot peppers and continue to fry for 5 more minutes.

■ Add the bell peppers and fry. When they are soft, replace the chicken, add the cilantro and tomatoes, and stir-fry for about 5 minutes on medium heat. Add a little water if needed. Test with a sharp knife that the chicken is cooked. Add salt to taste, and serve. It's nice with a squeeze of lemon juice over the top.

Note: In place of the spices, you can substitute 2 teaspoons of any type of curry paste.

Murog de Gama

CHICKEN DE GAMA

SERVES 4

The Portuguese were the first Europeans to invade India. Navigator Vasco da Gama landed in the south in 1498, seeking both converts to Christianity and spices. The latter he found in an unexpected way—he located one of the Arab spice exchange ports. At the time, the newly founded Moghul empire, under Babur, was busy establishing itself in the north, and this gave the Portuguese their foothold further south in Goa, where they established their capital. This recipe is in memory of the Portuguese arrival in Goa.

INGREDIENTS

1 spring chicken, about 2 1/2–3 pounds

3 tablespoons distilled vinegar

1 1/2 teaspoons salt

1/2 teaspoon freshly ground black pepper

1/4 cup Tamarind Purée (see page 34)

White flour for coating

4 tablespoons mustard oil or vegetable oil

2 1/2 tablespoons finely chopped garlic

1 1/2 tablespoons finely chopped ginger

3/4 cup finely chopped onion

1/2 teaspoon salt

Akhni Stock (see page 23) or water

Sugar and salt to taste

1 tablespoon finely chopped fresh cilantro leaves

SPICES

2-inch cinnamon stick, coarsely ground, *or* 2 teaspoons ground cinnamon

2 dried hot peppers, or 1/4 teaspoon ground red pepper (cayenne)

6 whole cloves

1 1/2 tablespoons freshly ground coriander

2 teaspoons freshly ground cumin

1/2 teaspoon black peppercorns

2 teaspoons turmeric

METHOD

■ Cut the chicken into 4 pieces (or 8 if you wish), skin it and wash in cold water. Dry well with a clean kitchen towel, put the pieces in a deep bowl, and sprinkle them with vinegar, 1 teaspoon salt, and the ground pepper, turning the pieces of meat over to coat them evenly. Pour the tamarind purée over the chicken, mix, and leave to marinate at room temperature for about 2 hours.

■ Drain the marinade from the chicken into the jar of an electric blender. Coat each piece of chicken with some flour so that it doesn't stick to the bottom of the frying pan.

■ Heat the oil in a large flat frying pan, and drop the chicken pieces in one by one. Turn them over frequently to brown them, and then transfer to a bowl. While frying, make sure that the heat is moderate or medium to low.

89

■ Add the garlic to the oil remaining in the pan and cook for 30 seconds, then add the ginger and cook for 30 seconds. Add the **Spices** and cook for 30 seconds, then the onions and 1/2 teaspoon salt. Mix well and stir-fry for about 5 minutes. Add a little Akhni stock or water as needed.

■ After 5 minutes, take the pan off the heat. With a spatula, scrape the mixture from the pan into the blender. Blend it well at high speed for about 1 minute.

■ Put the pan back on the heat, and pour in the blended mixture along with the pieces of chicken. Increase the heat and bring it to a boil, adding stock as required, and then reduce the heat to medium to low. Taste the sauce and if you find that it is a bit sour, add 2 teaspoons sugar or as necessary. Add salt to taste.

■ Simmer for 15 minutes and before switching off the heat, sprinkle the chopped cilantro over the curry and leave it, covered, for about 5 minutes before serving.

Murch Nawabi

CHICKEN COOKED WITH CREAM AND ALMONDS

SERVES 4

Lucknow is a Muslim city between Delhi and Bengal. It principally came to fame after the Moghuls departed, when it fell into the hands of an infamous succession of ten debauched, overweight Nawab-Wazirs; they reigned from the 1750s for a century in a haze of good living. Their harems and courtesan dancing girls are legendary. The final Nawab indulged himself to such excess that the British deposed him in 1856—a factor contributing to the Mutiny of 1857.

My own family was nearly wiped out in the uprising. My great-grand-father and his wife were massacred along with two thousand other British citizens. Their three-year-old daughter, Alice—my great-grandmother—was orphaned, and with no immediate family to go to was sent to the military school at Sanawar. She stayed there for nearly fifteen years until Alexander Lemmon, an official at the Government Telegraph department, went to the orphanage and chose her as his bride.

I'll never know whether my family ever tasted the following recipe, a particular delicacy of the Nawabs.

INGREDIENTS

6 tablespoons vegetable oil or ghee	1 tablespoon pistachio nuts
2 teaspoons Garlic Purée (see page 16)	2 tablespoons almonds
8 tablespoons Onion Purée (see page 17)	1 tablespoon golden raisins
2 tablespoons Curry Paste (storebought or homemade, page 20)	2 teaspoons ground cassia bark or cinnamon
1 1/2 pounds chicken breast, skinned and cubed	2 tablespoons chopped fresh cilantro leaves
Akhni Stock (see page 23) or water	4 fried eggs (optional)
2/3 cup light cream	

METHOD

■ Heat the oil in a *karahi* or wok, and stir-fry the garlic purée for 1 minute, then the onion purée for 3–4 minutes. Add the curry paste and stir-fry for another minute.

■ Add the chicken and stir-fry for 10 minutes. Use a little akhni stock or water as necessary to keep it from sticking.

■ Carefully add the cream, nuts, and golden raisins, the ground cassia bark, and the fresh cilantro.

■ Simmer for at least 10 more minutes, then serve. If you like, you can garnish each helping of this dish with a fried egg.

Pili-Pili Chicken

HOT PEPPER CHICKEN

SERVES 4

The origins of this dish go back to the Moors—the Arabs who by 900 AD were in control of a gigantic empire stretching from Spain to India. They used pepper to "heat" their food, but it was not until the Spanish discovered the New World in the sixteenth century that the hot pepper became an integral part of the food of the Middle East, the Orient, and, of course, India.

The common misconception about curry is that it is infested with hot peppers to an incendiary level, so it is quite remarkable to find that the hot pepper arrived late in the evolution of Indian cooking. Hot pepper heat must be taken in moderation by those not used to it. So, this is dish is not for the uninitiated. Adjust the heat level up or down to your taste, but do not omit the peppers altogether.

INGREDIENTS

4 tablespoons vegetable oil	2 tablespoons chopped fresh cilantro leaves
2 garlic cloves, chopped	2 fresh tomatoes, chopped
2-inch piece fresh ginger, chopped	Salt to taste
1/2 Spanish onion, peeled and chopped	SPICES 1 (WHOLE)
Water	1 teaspoon white cumin seeds
1/2 each of red, green and yellow bell peppers, chopped	1 teaspoon mustard seeds
3–6 fresh green hot peppers, chopped (to taste)	SPICES 2 (GROUND)
	1 teaspoon turmeric
1 1/2 pounds chicken breast, skinned and cubed	1 tablespoon Mild Curry Powder (store-bought or homemade, see page 12)

METHOD

■ Heat the oil and fry **Spices 1**, the garlic, ginger, and onion for just 1 minute each.

■ Add **Spices 2** and a tiny bit of water just to prevent sticking. Add the sweet and hot peppers and the chicken, and stir-fry for 10 minutes.

■ Add the cilantro and tomatoes, and stir-fry for a minimum of 5 minutes more. Check that the chicken is cooked through (cut a large piece in half) and if so serve at once. This dish loses freshness if it stands around.

Chicken Tikka Masala or Rezala

CHICKEN PIECES IN TANDOORI SAUCE

SERVES 4

I use three methods for achieving tandoori/tikkas. First, for small quantities, I use the grill; second, for large quantities, I use the oven; and I have recently been experimenting with a third method, stir-frying, which is easier to control than the grill—the chicken cooks more evenly and does not burn so easily. My method of stir-frying also imparts a rich color while also searing the chicken, and if you want to blacken the edges (it does add a little to the effect and taste) at the end of the stir-fry phase, just heat under the broiler for a few seconds.

Putting tandoori-cooked items into a rich red tomato sauce which uses spare tandoori marinade is a relatively recent restaurateur's invention, and it has become the diners' favorite dish. The dish is encountered under several names—*tikka masala*, *tandoori masala*, *tandoori*, or *tikka makhani* (butter) or *makhanwalla* (cooked in butter) or *choosa masala* or *rezala*. Indeed, some restaurants offer most of their curries combined with the tandoori/tikka sauce so you get *bhoona tikka masala* or *pasanda tikka masala*, etc.

INGREDIENTS

TIKKA/TANDOORI

1 1/2 pounds chicken breast, skinned and cubed, *or* a 2 1/2–3 pound spring chicken, skinned and quartered

Juice of 2 lemons

1 cup Tandoori Marinade (see page 31)

SAUCE

6 tablespoons vegetable oil

6 tablespoons Curry Masala Sauce (see page 22)

2 teaspoons Tandoori Paste (see page 31)

2 tablespoons Tandoori Marinade (see page 31)

2 teaspoons tomato purée

1/2 green bell pepper, seeded and chopped

1–4 fresh green hot peppers, chopped (to taste)

1 tomato, chopped

2 tablespoons plain yogurt

2 tablespoons chopped fresh cilantro leaves (or purée)

1 tablespoon ground almonds

1 tablespoon light cream

1 teaspoon sugar (optional)

Salt to taste

METHOD

■ In the case of a quartered chicken, cut short, shallow slashes on the flesh. This gives an interesting appearance to the finished dish, and a greater surface area for the marinade to adhere to.

■ Rub the flesh with the lemon juice and let stand for 15 minutes. This degreases and tenderizes the meat, preparing it for the marinade.

■ Shake off excess lemon juice (reserve any left, to use later in the sauce) and, using a deep bowl, thoroughly coat the chicken flesh with the tandoori marinade. Ensure the marinade reaches all parts generously. Let stand in the refrigerator overnight, but preferably for 24 or even 30 hours—a minimum of 6 hours. The longer you leave it, the deeper the marinade penetrates (but for the instant method, see below).

■ *Cooking the Chicken* To cook in the tandoor or over a barbecue, place the pieces or quarters on skewers. Place the skewers over the coals. Cook for 15 minutes, turning once or twice. Test for doneness, then remove.

To broil, arrange the pieces on a broiler rack and place the pan about 6 inches below the heat, which should be set at medium-high. Cook as above.

To bake, place the pieces on an oven tray—don't cram them together, or they won't cook evenly. Place in an oven preheated to 325°F and cook for 15–20 minutes.

When I forgot to do even a 6-hour marinating, an instant stir-frying to infuse flavor in the *tikka* has worked for me very satisfactorily. Simply coat the tikkas in the marinade. Heat some oil in the *karahi* or wok, and stir-fry with about 4 tablespoons of excess marinade. Place the tikkas in the *karahi* and stir-fry for 15 minutes.

■ For the sauce, heat the oil in a *karahi*, and simmer the curry sauce, paste, marinade, and tomato purée. After 2–3 minutes add the sweet and hot peppers and tomato, and continue to simmer for 5 minutes or so.

■ Add all the remaining ingredients, and mix. When simmering, add the chicken, and stir through. Serve when hot.

Anarkali Bahar

SIZZLING TANDOORI CHICKEN

SERVES 4

The chicken pieces are tandoori marinated and baked, then they're dry-fried and brought sizzling to the table. To achieve the smoky sizzle, you need cast-iron sizzler platters or *karahis*. If you don't have these, simply serve non-sizzling. It will still taste the same.

INGREDIENTS

1 1/2 pounds chicken breast, skinned and boned	3 tablespoons mustard or canola oil
1 Spanish onion, peeled and chopped	Juice of 1 lemon
1 green bell pepper, seeded and chopped	Salt to taste
2 tomatoes, chopped	**SPICES**
Vegetable oil	1 teaspoon dried mint
2 limes	2 teaspoons dry fenugreek leaf
MARINADE	2 tablespoons Curry Paste (storebought or homemade, see page 20)
2 teaspoons Garlic Purée (see page 16)	1 tablespoon Tandoori Paste (see page 31)
1 teaspoon Ginger Purée (see page 16)	2 tablespoons chopped fresh cilantro leaves
2/3 cup plain yogurt	

METHOD

■ Cube the chicken breast, and mix together the marinade ingredients and **Spices**. Combine, and leave for a minimum of 6 hours, a maximum of 30 hours in the refrigerator.

■ Cook the chicken pieces on a skewer over charcoal, under a broiler at medium heat, or bake in the oven at 325°F for 15–20 minutes. You could also stir-fry them.

■ Meanwhile take four cast-iron *karahis* (*baltis* in the Midlands) and heat them on the stove. In them, stir-fry the onion, pepper, and tomatoes in a little oil.

■ Divide the chicken between the *karahis* and mix. Just before serving, squeeze some lime juice on the *karahis,* which, providing they're hot enough, will sizzle and give off a lot of smoke. Using tongs, serve at once.

Kaeng Keo Wan Gai

THAI GREEN CHICKEN CURRY

SERVES 4

Thai curry should have that distinctive fragrance that comes from kaffir lime leaves (*makrut*) and lemongrass (*takrai*), coupled with the background tastes of shrimp paste (*kapi*) and fish sauce (*nam-pla*). The curry becomes more distinctive with the use of *kha* or galengal, which I have specified in the recipe below for use in its fresh root form; if unobtainable, use a mixture of fresh ginger (to which it is related) and galengal powder.

INGREDIENTS

4 tablespoons vegetable oil

1 3/4 cups thick coconut milk

1 1/2 pounds chicken breast, skinned, boned, and diced

3 tablespoons *nam-pla* (fish sauce)

2 tablespoons sugar

2 ounces large eggplant slices (*makua paw*) (about 1/4 medium-size eggplant)

1 ounce baby eggplant (*makua puang*)

1/2 green bell pepper, seeded and thinly sliced

Sprig of basil leaves

1 large fresh kaffir lime leaf, finely chopped

CURRY PASTE

1 1/2 green bell peppers, seeded and coarsely chopped

2–7 green hot peppers, chopped (to taste)

1-inch piece fresh galengal (*kha*) or 1/2 teaspoon powder

8 tablespoons Onion Purée (see page 17) *or* finely chopped shallots

2 teaspoons Garlic Purée (see page 16)

1 teaspoon ground coriander

1 tablespoon fresh lemongrass leaves, finely chopped, *or* 1 teaspoon powder

1 tablespoon *nam-pla* (fish sauce)

1 teaspoon *kapi* (shrimp paste)

1 teaspoon chopped fresh cilantro leaves

6–7 fresh or dried kaffir lime leaves

METHOD

■ Blend all the curry paste ingredients in the blender or food processor to a thick paste.

■ Heat the oil in a large pan, and stir-fry the curry paste with a little coconut milk for about 5 minutes. Add the chicken pieces and stir-fry for about 10 minutes.

■ Add the remaining coconut milk, the fish sauce, sugar, and eggplant, plus some water if necessary to enable the items to boil.

■ Simmer for 5 minutes, then add the green pepper, basil, and lime leaf. Stir in and serve promptly.

Stuffed Baked Glazed Quail

SERVES 4

Quail are quite common in northern India, where quail recipes are especially beloved by the ex-Maharajas. This recipe is an invention of mine, combining several Indian concepts. You need boned quail—your butcher can get them boned, or you can do it yourself, but it's fiddly. The boned quail are then marinated tandoori-style for 24 hours. After being stuffed, they are baked in the oven, glazed, and finished under the broiler. They can be served with salad and make a fine starter or main dish.

INGREDIENTS

4 boned, prepared quail (keep the skin on)

MARINADE (WELL MIXED)

1/3 to 1/3 cup plain yogurt

3 teaspoons Tandoori Paste (see page 31)

1 teaspoon dried mint

1 teaspoon garlic powder

STUFFING

4–6 tablespoons cooked rice

GLAZE

4 tablespoons clear honey

2 teaspoons Worcestershire sauce

METHOD

■ Put the quail and the marinade together in a nonreactive bowl with a lid. Use your fingers to ensure thorough blending. Place in the refrigerator for 24 hours.

■ The next day, preheat the oven to 375° F, and remove the quail from the marinade. Open them out and spread them on a work surface.

■ Mix into the cooked cold rice—better if slightly glutinous—a small amount of leftover marinade. Take about 1–1 1/2 tablespoons rice, compress it, and gently fold the quail around it so that it resumes its boned shape. Tuck the flaps of skin and the legs in and gently squeeze them into shape. Place them breast-side up on an oven tray. They don't need trussing providing you have got a firm shapely quail. Pour any remaining marinade over each quail.

■ Place the oven tray in the oven, and bake for 15 minutes.

■ About 4 minutes before taking them out of the oven, preheat the broiler and a burner on the stove. Mix the honey and Worcestershire sauce in a small pan and heat.

■ Take the quail from the oven and pour the glaze carefully over them, ensuring it covers all the exposed flesh.

■ Place under the broiler for minute or two to finish off. Serve hot or cold.

Note: A more elaborate stuffing could be a *Nargissi kofta ke bahar* filling (page 47). Simply cover a hard-boiled quail egg with the meat mixture uncooked to the same size as the rice (about chicken-egg size), and bake and glaze as above (without the rice, of course).

Batare Masala

CURRIED QUAIL

SERVES 4

INGREDIENTS

4 whole quail (preferably boned)	10 cloves
2 tablespoons Curry Paste (storebought or homemade, see page 20)	4-inch piece of cassia bark or cinnamon stick
1/3 cup plain yogurt	2 teaspoons white cumin seeds
SAUCE	1 teaspoon fennel seeds
2 tablespoons ghee	1/2 teaspoon black cumin seeds
8 tablespoons Curry Masala Sauce (see page 22)	1/2–2 teaspoons ground red pepper (cayenne)
1 1/2 tablespoons chickpea flour (*besan*)	1/2 teaspoon mango powder
Akhni Stock (see page 23) or water	GARNISHES
1/4 cup whipping cream	4 sheets silver leaf (*vark*) (see page 144)
Salt to taste	2 tablespoons sliced almonds
SPICES	1 tablespoon chopped fresh cilantro leaves
1 teaspoon turmeric	
6 brown cardamoms	

98

METHOD

■ Clean the quail, then prick them all over. Mix the curry paste with the yogurt in a large bowl, then cover the quail thoroughly. Let marinate in the refrigerator for a minimum of 6, a maximum of 30, hours.

■ To cook, preheat the oven to 325°F. Place the quail and their marinade on an oven tray and bake for 15 minutes.

■ Meanwhile, make the sauce. Heat the ghee in a *karahi* or wok, and stir-fry the **Spices** for 1 minute. Add the curry masala sauce and heat until simmering.

■ Mix the flour with the water to make a paste. Add it to the *karahi*, and as it thickens, add akhni stock or water to keep it from becoming too thick. Add the cream, and some salt to taste.

■ Take the quail from the oven—they should be cooked, with the marinade well caramelized. If not, finish under the broiler. Place the quail in the *karahi*, and simmer for 5 minutes.

■ Garnish with silver leaf (page 144), and place the sliced almonds and chopped cilantro on top of this.

Goan Roast Duckling

SERVES 2

If you believed that marinated roast duckling was the sole preserve of the Pekinese Chinese, then I urge you to sample this recipe. Using the standard tandoori marinade, the whole duckling is baked to produce a crispy, deep red, very tasty dish. Optionally, it could be stuffed with cooked rice or an apple, but I prefer to leave it unstuffed to allow the drippings (which can be used for future curry cooking) to escape easily into the drip tray.

For four people use two 3 1/2-pound ducks, and more marinade. Use the same marinating and cooking times.

INGREDIENTS

1 whole duckling, approximately 3 1/2 pounds	Juice of 2 lemons
	1 recipe Tandoori Marinade (see page 31)

METHOD

- Clean the duckling inside and out. Poke a sharp knife all over and deep into the duck, then rub in the lemon juice and let stand for half an hour in a deep bowl.

- Strain and keep the leftover lemon juice. Now work the tandoori marinade into the duck, and leave it to stand in the bowl for at least 6 hours.

- Preheat the oven to 350°F. While it is warming, remove the duck from the bowl, shaking off any excess marinade, and place on an oven tray. Smear some of the excess marinade back onto the duck, enough to give it an even coating. Place the duck in the oven. The total roasting time will be about 1 3/4 hours (allowing 30 minutes per pound).

- After about 45 minutes, remove the duck and baste it with the remaining marinade. Return to the oven, and after 1 1/2 hours pierce the plump part of the leg. When it is cooked, the fluid that runs out will be clear; if not replace for longer. The marinade will have caramelized into a fantastic crispy coating. Place in a low oven to rest for 15 minutes, then cut into two servings, a half duck per person.

Sri Lankan Duck

SERVES 4

Duck is enjoyed in Sri Lanka and suits this recipe very well. Ask for duck breasts.

INGREDIENTS

4 duck breasts, about 8 ounces each	Salt to taste
Water	SPICES (WHOLE)
4 tablespoons fat rendered from the duck	2 teaspoons coriander seeds
2 teaspoons Garlic Purée (see page 16)	1 teaspoon cumin seeds
1 tablespoon Ginger Purée (see page 16)	1 teaspoon fennel seeds
8 tablespoons Onion Purée (see page 17)	1/2 teaspoon fenugreek seeds
3 1/2 ounces coconut cream	1 small piece cassia bark or cinnamon stick
1 tablespoon brown sugar	
3/4 cup tomato soup (about 1/2 can)	1/2 teaspoon cloves
1 tablespoon any vinegar	1/2 teaspoon green cardamoms

METHOD

■ Preheat the oven to 375°F, and place the duck breasts on a rack on an oven tray. When the oven is hot, put the tray in, and roast for 25 minutes.

■ Meanwhile, in the same oven, place the **Spices** on another oven tray and roast for 3 minutes. Cool, then grind to a fine dark powder. Make into a paste using a little water.

■ Remove the duck tray from the oven, and strain off the fat. Decide whether you want to use the skin. If yes, decide whether it needs more cooking to get it totally crispy. if it does, pull it away from the breast and return to the oven—if you don't want to use the skin, discard it.

■ Heat the rendered duck fat in a *karahi* or wok, and stir-fry the garlic, ginger, and onion purées together for 4 minutes. Add the spice paste and stir-fry for another 5 minutes. Add the coconut cream, sugar, tomato soup, and vinegar. Stir-fry until simmering.

■ Cut the duck breasts into thin slices. Place them and the fried mixture into a casserole dish and return to the oven to finish off for about 20 more minutes. Add salt to taste.

FISH

▲▲▲▲▲▲▲▲▲▲▲▲▲▲▲▲▲

I quite enjoy fish when I remember it exists, but my repertoire is, frankly, limited to a few old favorites—cod, sole, and trout. Yet a good fishmonger's slab is a work of art, and a discussion with the experts is an education. I visited a large supermarket recently, and this is what they had for sale, fresh, that day: bream, haddock, hake, halibut, herring, John Dory, lemon sole, mackerel, pike, trout, salmon, sea bass, sprats, turbot, and whiting. They also had the following frozen fish: red snapper, red mullet, sardines, shark steaks, swordfish steaks, tuna steaks, and whitebait.

And that was not all. Their shellfish department was equally impressive, with fresh and frozen items including shrimp, clams, crab, crayfish, lobster, monkfish, scallops, mussels, oysters, octopus, and squid.

I mention this not because I have recipes for all of these items, but to show the fantastic wealth of fish and shellfish from which you can choose. You can easily substitute one fish or shellfish for another.

Grilled Spiced Trout

SERVES 4
AS A MAIN
COURSE,
8 AS A
STARTER

The emperor Jahangir built his famous Kashmiri gardens in the 1600s. In their pools, he kept large trout. In their noses, he put gold rings. Their descendants still swim in these pools—sadly without their rings.

Fresh trout is delightful when cooked with spices, but it *must* be fresh. The spicing itself can be very light indeed, as in this delicious recipe.

INGREDIENTS

4 fresh trout, about 12 ounces each

SPICE MARINADE

1 teaspoon turmeric

1 teaspoon ground cumin

1 teaspoon ground black pepper

4 tablespoons chopped fresh cilantro leaves

3 tablespoons mustard or peanut oil

1 teaspoon salt

METHOD

■ Gut and carefully wash the trout clean, then dry them.

■ Mix the marinade ingredients together and coat the trout thoroughly, leaving it to absorb the flavors for about 1 hour.

■ Broil or fry the fish—about 10 minutes—and serve at once on a bed of lettuce with lemon wedges and onion rings.

Tandoori Trout or Mackerel

SERVES 4

This is another way to cook trout, using a tandoori marinade. You can use a commercial tandoori paste for this, but it's better still to make your own (page 31). Once again, serve for four as a main course, or eight as a starter.

INGREDIENTS

4 fresh trout, about 12 ounces each (or mackerel or salmon)	1 recipe Tandoori Marinade (see page 31)

■ Proceed exactly as for grilled spiced trout on page 103, using the tandoori marinade. Serve similarly.

Patrani Machli

LEAF (OR FOIL) BAKED FISH

SERVES 4 AS
A STARTER

There is no other dish like this in the entire culinary repertoire of the subcontinent. Created by the Parsee community of Bombay, it is a chunky fish (*machli*) coated with green herb paste and wrapped in a banana or patra leaf and steamed. Pomfret is the fish the Parsees use, but as it is not very easy to get hold of, it is quite acceptable to use alternatives such as cod or other fleshy white fish. Banana leaves are also hard to come by, so this method uses aluminum foil. All this sounds complicated, but in fact the dish is really quite straightforward.

I like to serve this as a starter with no accompaniments, to get the most out of the fabulous flavors.

INGREDIENTS

4 pieces filleted cod steak, about 8 ounces each	2 bunches fresh cilantro, leaves plus tender stalks
3 tablespoons mustard oil or vegetable oil	1–4 green hot peppers, coarsely chopped (to taste)
2 tablespoons any vinegar	1 garlic clove
COATING	1 tablespoon flaked coconut, ground to a powder
1/2 Spanish onion, peeled and coarsely chopped	

COATING (CONT)

1 teaspoon sugar
1/2 teaspoon salt
1 teaspoon ground cumin
Juice of 1 lemon

GARNISHES

Chopped fresh cilantro
Lemon wedges

METHOD

■ Grind all the coating ingredients together in a blender. The paste should be of a thick porridge-like consistency. (If it is too thin, put in a strainer to drain; and if too thick, add a little water.)

■ Lay each piece of fish on a large piece of foil, then cover completely with paste, using up all the paste. Wrap the fish pieces tightly in the foil.

■ Meanwhile, put the oil and vinegar in an oven tray, and into an oven preheated to 375°F. When hot, put the foiled fish into the tray and bake for 20 minutes.

■ To serve, carefully unwrap and discard the foil. The coating should have adhered to the fish and it should be quite moist. Pour all or some of the liquid in the pan over the dish. Garnish with fresh cilantro and lemon wedges.

Machher Jhol or Maachli Jhal

BENGALI FISH

SERVES 4

The River Ganges is sacred to Hindus. Not only is it one of the world's largest rivers, it also contains a huge variety of freshwater fish, nowhere more prolific than at its tributaries and estuaries. Here the Ganges delta and its offshoot, the Hougli, divide Bengal from Bangladesh—but the cooking is much the same, and fish figures prominently.

INGREDIENTS

1 teaspoon turmeric	6 tablespoons Curry Masala Sauce (see page 22)
1/2 teaspoon salt	3/4 cup Akhni Stock (see page 23) or water
1 1/2 pounds halibut or other firm white fish fillets	GARNISH
4 tablespoons mustard or peanut oil	1 tablespoon chopped fresh cilantro leaves or saffron strands
1 teaspoon *Panch Phoran* (see page 36)	

METHOD

■ Mix the turmeric and salt into a runny paste with a tiny drop of water, and spread over the fish. Traditionally, this is supposed both to enhance the flavor of the fish and reduce the odor during cooking.

■ Heat the oil in a large pan, then fry the panch phoran for 1 minute. Add the fish pieces, and fry each side for 2 minutes, turning once. Add the curry masala sauce, shake the pan to mix, and simmer for 2 minutes.

■ Add enough akhni stock or water to just cover the fish. Simmer for 10 minutes, always shaking the pan rather than stirring, which can break up the fish.

■ Remove the fish from the pan carefully, and serve with a little of the sauce. Garnish with fresh cilantro or saffron.

Jingha Hara Masala

SHRIMP IN GREEN HERBS

SERVES 4

I was staying south of Madras. On the first night I was there, I watched the sun set over the sea, and as the last orange rays faded, about twenty tiny *dhow*-like boats with chugging engines appeared from a township about a mile down the beach. They had small sails and, as the sky went purple, little twinkling oil lights were lit on each boat. The fish boats spread out and anchored about three miles out. They stayed immobile, twinkling all night. I got up early in the morning just as the sun was rising. When I got to the village, the boats were being roped up and the entire population—women, children, and old folk—were all pulling ropes, spreading sails and nets out on the sand to dry, and offering huge baskets to the fishermen to put the catch in. The contents of these baskets were amazing, with all sorts of sea creatures, but it was the shrimp that caught my eye—thousands of them, tiny and transparent. As I watched, two local chefs appeared and were handed a basket each. We walked back to their kitchen together and they promised to cook some of those fresh shrimp for lunch. This is what they cooked.

INGREDIENTS

2 pounds tiny shrimp (200–300 to the pound)	1 tablespoon Green Masala Paste (see page 21)
3 tablespoons ghee or vegetable oil	1 tablespoon chopped fresh mint leaves
Salt	2–6 green hot peppers, coarsely chopped (to taste)
Green food coloring (optional)	1 green bell pepper, seeded and coarsely chopped
PASTE	2 tablespoons grated fresh coconut
1 Spanish onion, peeled and coarsely chopped	
2 tablespoons chopped fresh cilantro leaves *or* Cilantro Purée (see page 18)	

METHOD

- For the paste, blend all the ingredients into a paste/purée.

- Peel, wash, or thaw the shrimp.

- In a frying pan or wok, heat the ghee or vegetable oil to medium. Add the shrimp and fry for 2–3 minutes, then add the paste.

- Simmer for about 10–15 minutes. Add a little green food coloring if you want a more vivid green color.

107

Chingree in Coconut

COCONUT SHRIMP

SERVES 4

This recipe comes from Bangladesh, where the language is Bengali. *Chingree* means shrimp and is very similar to the Hindi word *jinga* or *jingri*. Nowhere do shrimps or prawns grow bigger, more succulent or more tasty. Use jumbo size shrimp (about 8–12 to the pound) or larger and simply remove the head and the vein.

INGREDIENTS

2 pounds shrimp	3/4 cup milk
2 tablespoons vegetable oil	Juice of 1 lemon
1 tablespoon black mustard seeds	1–3 fresh hot peppers, chopped (to taste)
1–4 tablespoons Garlic Purée (see page 16)	Salt to taste
2 teaspoons Ginger Purée (see page 16)	SPICES (ROASTED AND GROUND)
1 medium onion, peeled and cut into rings	2 teaspoons coriander
	1/4 teaspoon fenugreek
1/4 cup coconut cream	1 teaspoon black peppercorns
1 tablespoon flaked coconut, ground to a powder	6 curry leaves
	1-2 teaspoons water

METHOD

- De-head, shell, devein, wash, and dry the shrimp.

- Make a paste of the **Spices**, using a little water.

- Heat the oil, fry the mustard seeds, the garlic purée, and ginger purée, then the spice paste, each for 1 minute, one after the other.

- Add the onion rings and fry until translucent, then add the two coconuts and the milk. Stir-fry for 2 minutes, then add the lemon juice, hot peppers, and salt.

- When simmering, add the shrimp. Stir-fry for 10 minutes, then serve.

King Prawn Masala

SERVES 4

I've met a dish like this in various parts of India, including Bombay and Madras. This recipe uses large shrimp (about 16–20 to the pound), but you can use any size you wish.

INGREDIENTS

2 pounds shrimp	Salt to taste
4 tablespoons ghee or vegetable oil	1 tablespoon chopped fresh cilantro leaves
1 teaspoon Garlic Purée (see page 16)	1 tablespoon Garam Masala (storebought or homemade, see page 35)
1 teaspoon Ginger Purée (see page 16)	SPICES
8 tablespoons Onion Purée (see page 17)	1/2 teaspoon turmeric
1–4 green hot peppers (to taste)	1/2 teaspoon ground red pepper (cayenne)
6 medium tomatoes	

METHOD

- Shell and devein the shrimp.

- While heating the oil, mix together the garlic, ginger, and onion purées in a blender with the hot peppers, and blend again.

- Stir-fry this purée in the hot oil for 5 minutes until golden, then add the **Spices**. Fry for 2 more minutes.

- Meanwhile, purée the tomatoes, then add them to your pan. Stir-fry until the mixture reduces a little—about 10 minutes—and becomes a darker red.

- Add the shrimp and simmer for about 10 minutes, before salting to taste.

- Toss in the chopped cilantro and garam masala. Stir-fry for 3–5 minutes, then serve.

Jeera Prawn

SHRIMP STIR-FRIED IN CUMIN SEEDS

SERVES 4

A little spice can go a long way, for all that is used to make this an astonishingly tasty dish is cumin seeds and turmeric. *Jeera Prawn* makes an excellent starter (halve the quantities given here) or main course, and takes less than 15 minutes to prepare and cook.

INGREDIENTS

1 1/2 pounds shrimp in brine, or thawed frozen, or fresh	2 teaspoons Ginger Purée (see page 16)
6 tablespoons mustard or peanut oil	1 1/2 teaspoons turmeric
2 tablespoons whole white cumin seeds	1 red bell pepper, cut into julienne strips
2 red onions, *or* 1 Spanish onion, peeled and finely chopped	1–4 green hot peppers, finely chopped (to taste)
2 teaspoons Garlic Purée (see page 16)	1-3 teaspoons water or brine from shrimp
	Salt and pepper

METHOD

■ Prepare the shrimp, shelling, draining, drying, etc. as appropriate.

■ Heat the oil to hot in a *karahi* or wok, and fry the cumin seeds for 30 seconds—until they pop. Then add the onion and fry until it starts to crisp. Add the garlic purée, ginger purée, and turmeric, stir-fry for 2 minutes, then add the sweet and hot peppers. Add a very little water or some of the brine to prevent sticking.

■ After 2 more minutes, add the shrimp and simmer for enough time to get them good and hot, about 5 minutes (no longer or shrimp become rubbery). Add salt and pepper to taste. Serve at once.

Lobster Korma

SERVES 4

A century after the Portuguese, the English discovered India and in 1608 obtained the permission of the Moghuls to trade. They set up their first docks at Surat (north of Bombay), but they had it in mind to establish trading stations around India, in areas outside direct Moghul control. They chose three virgin sites with good potential anchorages. Factories came first, then townships, and finally armies to defend them. Madras was established in 1640, Bombay in 1674, and Calcutta in 1690. Calcutta was the British capital of India until 1911, and with its abundance of seaboard and river estuaries, the area has always been notable for fish and seafood.

INGREDIENTS

4 lobsters or crawfish, about 1 pound each	MARINADE
3 tablespoons ghee	1/3 cup plain yogurt
6 tablespoons Onion Purée (see page 17)	1 tablespoon Garlic Purée (see page 16)
3/4–1 cup Akhni Stock (see page 23)	1 tablespoon Ginger Purée (see page 16)
1 teaspoon saffron	SPICES
1 tablespoon chopped fresh cilantro leaves	2-inch piece cassia bark or cinnamon stick
Salt to taste	6 green cardamoms

METHOD

■ Boil the lobsters, if fresh, for 15 minutes. If frozen, thaw. When cool, cleave the shells in two and pick out all the flesh. Chop it into bite-sized pieces. (Discard the shells or use them to serve the *korma* in.)

■ Mix the marinade ingredients in a large bowl. Place the lobster pieces in the marinade and leave for 1 hour.

■ After an hour, heat the ghee and stir-fry the onion purée for 5 minutes. Add the spices and the akhni stock, and heat to simmering.

■ Add the lobster, and cook for 10 minutes. Add the saffron, fresh cilantro, and salt to taste. Mix and serve.

VEGETABLES

▲▲▲▲▲▲▲▲▲▲▲▲▲▲▲▲▲▲

Southern India has been mostly vegetarian since the Dravidian tribes occupied it many thousands of years ago. Vegetarianism in the north of India came much later with the establishment of the Hindu religion in around 1000 BC with the veneration of the cow. Of today's Indian population of some 700 million, probably in excess of 75 percent are vegetarian.

Nowhere on earth are vegetables cooked more effectively than in India. Spicing and curry-making techniques elevate humble ingredients to great dishes. Take lentils, for example. By the addition of a few spices, ordinary red lentils are as tasty as any curry, and served with rice or bread make a very economical and nutritiously complete meal.

I have selected a varied range of recipes which incorporate many different vegetables and techniques. Bear in mind also that many of the recipes in the previous chapters can be adapted to your choice of vegetable.

A trip to an Asian-community produce stand is an amazing experience. There you will see tray upon tray of unfamiliar vegetables of all types. These and many others are everyday items to the Indian cook, but most of us do not have access to such produce. In any case, much of it is very bitter or unpalatable to the Western palate, so I have excluded the real oddities from my recipes.

Many of the dishes following can be served as a vegetarian main course. If required as a vegetable accompaniment only, simply halve the ingredients.

Vegetable Bhajee

SERVES 4
AS A MAIN
COURSE

This is the standard vegetable curry—*bhajee* meaning cooked vegetables—and it appears on the menu of most curry houses. It has no specific regional origin in the subcontinent so there are many variations of the dish, but in general terms it is any combination of vegetables in a curry sauce—potatoes, cauliflower, carrot, and peas being the most commonly encountered. It can be easily spoiled by overcooking the vegetables—and as vegetables take different lengths of time to boil, it is important to pre-cook them individually first.

INGREDIENTS

1 1/2 pounds vegetables made up as
    follows:
    potatoes, peeled and cubed; carrots,
    sliced; frozen peas, and frozen beans

2 tablespoons sunflower oil

1 tablespoon Curry Paste (storebought
    or homemade, see page 20)

12 tablespoons Onion Purée (see page 17)

1 tablespoon chopped fresh cilantro
    leaves

Salt to taste

Akhni Stock (see page 23) or water

METHOD

■ Boil the vegetables separately to near readiness—crisp but not mushy. If the vegetables are to be used later, rinse them in cold water and strain.

■ Heat the oil and stir-fry the curry paste for 1 minute, then the onion purée for 5 minutes. When simmering, add in the vegetables followed by the fresh cilantro and salt to taste. Add water or stock to get as runny a consistency as you want.

■ Serve promptly.

Vegan Bhajee

SERVES 4
AS A MAIN
COURSE

Vegan describes people who are true vegetarians. This means they eat no dairy products at all, including butter, ghee, yogurt, and eggs. You can use any vegetables of your choice for this dish, but the following is a tasty combination.

INGREDIENTS

1 1/2 pounds vegetables, made up as follows:
parsnip, peeled and cubed; sweet potatoes, peeled and cubed; zucchini, sliced; and frozen peas

2 tablespoons sunflower oil

1 teaspoon turmeric

1 teaspoon Garlic Purée (see page 16)

12 tablespoons Onion Purée (see page 17)

1 tablespoons Curry Paste (storebought or homemade, see page 20)

1 tablespoon chopped fresh cilantro leaves

Salt to taste

Akhni Stock (see page 23) or water

METHOD

■ Cook everything as in the previous recipe, stir-frying the turmeric for 20 seconds, then the garlic purée for 1 minute, the onion purée for 3 minutes, and the paste for 1 minute.

Bindi Bhajee

OKRA CURRY

SERVES 4
AS A MAIN
COURSE

Bindis are okra. They are rather difficult to cook. The first factor is careful selection. It is usually better to choose smaller ones—the large ones are often scaly. To prepare them, wash carefully. Dry them, then cut off the point and trim off the stalk. Do not cook them in water, otherwise they ooze sap while cooking. It's most unpleasant, and unfortunately this is one of those dishes which many get wrong. It can only be successful if it is cooked fresh. A microwave is the best of all, giving lovely crisp results.

In Bengali, this dish is called *dherosh chach-chori*, and in the south of India *vendaika.*

INGREDIENTS

1 1/2 pounds okra	
6 tablespoons mustard or peanut oil	
2 teaspoons mustard seeds	
4 tablespoons chopped onion (preferable red ones for flavor and color)	
Juice of 1 lemon	
1 tablespoon brown sugar	
2 tomatoes, finely chopped	
1 tablespoon chopped fresh cilantro leaves	
Salt to taste	

SPICES 1 (GROUND)

1/2 teaspoon turmeric

1 teaspoon cumin

1 teaspoon coriander

1/2 teaspoon ground red pepper (cayenne)

1 teaspoon garlic powder

1-3 teaspoons water

SPICES 2

1 teaspoon ground cassia bark or cinnamon

1/2 teaspoon green cardamom seeds (not pods)

METHOD

- Carefully wash the okra, then dry them. Cut off the pointed tip and the stalk and discard.

- Mix **Spices 1** into a paste with a little water.

- Heat the oil in a *karahi* or wok. Stir-fry the mustard seeds until they pop, about 1 minute, then add the spice paste and fry for 2 minutes, then the onion for 3 minutes.

- Meanwhile, chop the okra into 1-inch pieces, add them to the *karahi*, and gently toss for 5 minutes.

- Add the lemon juice, sugar, tomato, **Spices 2**, and fresh cilantro.

- Stir-fry carefully for 5 more minutes. If the okra were tender to start with, they are now cooked perfectly. Add salt to taste.

- Serve at once. Do not store or freeze this dish—it will become sappy and mushy.

Mushroom Bhajee

SERVES 4
as a side

One of my favorite dishes, but only if the mushrooms are absolutely fresh—white button ones are best. Do not stew them—in fact, simply add them whole or quartered, or thinly sliced in a food processor, coat them with the hot sauce and serve at once. This dish does not keep or freeze.

INGREDIENTS

1 1/2 pounds mushrooms	
3 tablespoons vegetable oil (sesame or sunflower)	
2 teaspoons Garlic Purée (see page 16)	
6 tablespoons Onion Purée (see page 17)	
Akhni Stock (see page 23) or water	
1–2 fresh hot peppers, chopped (to taste)	
1 tablespoon chopped fresh cilantro leaves	
Salt to taste	

SPICES (GROUND)

1 teaspoon coriander
1 teaspoon cumin
2 teaspoons paprika
1/2 teaspoon turmeric

METHOD

■ Wash the mushrooms, and only peel them if they look as though they need it. Leave whole, quarter, or thinly slice them.

■ Heat the oil and fry the garlic purée at quite high heat for just 1 minute. Add the onion purée and fry for about 3–5 minutes. They should be golden brown.

■ Make a paste of the **Spices** with a little vegetable stock or water, and add to the onion. Fry for another 5 minutes, then add sufficient water or stock to obtain a thick but fluid mixture. When it is simmering, add the mushrooms and the fresh hot peppers and cilantro. When they are hot, they are ready to serve—and the fresher the better. Add salt to taste.

Sag Wala

SPINACH CURRY

SERVES 4
AS A MAIN
DISH

S*ag* means spinach and *wala* means cooked (it also means a tradesman, and the *punka wala*, for example, was the servant who operated the ceiling fan in the old days). This dish is commonly called *sag bhajee*.

INGREDIENTS

1 1/2 pounds fresh or frozen spinach	4 tablespoons Curry Masala Sauce (see page 22)
6 tablespoons ghee or vegetable oil	Salt to taste
2–6 garlic cloves, thinly sliced	SPICES
1/2 Spanish onion, peeled and finely chopped	1/2 teaspoon black cumin seeds
1–4 fresh green hot peppers, chopped (to taste)	1 teaspoon white cumin seeds

METHOD

■ Wash the grit out of the spinach leaves if using fresh, or thaw if using frozen leaf. Chop it up. Blanch fresh leaves in boiling water for 3–4 minutes. Strain.

■ Heat the ghee and stir-fry the garlic for 1 minute, then the **Spices** for 1 minute. Add the onion and fresh hot pepper and stir-fry for another 3 minutes.

■ Add the sauce and, when simmering, add the spinach and salt to taste. Briskly stir around until hot. Serve or keep warm. It will freeze, but it is safe to do so only with fresh spinach.

Navrattan Korma

NINE MILDLY CURRIED VEGETABLES

SERVES 4

Nine vegetables (excluding garlic, ginger, onion, and cilantro) is a lot, so you may wish to make this dish for special occasions. It is a good party dish, particularly if you choose and cut your vegetables to provide interesting contrasts of color and shapes.

The number nine is very significant. Akbar was perhaps the greatest Moghul emperor, and during his reign in the sixteenth century he gave the most talented men in the empire special places at court. They were nine. Included in this elite club were not only Akbar's heads of state and his generals, there was his most fabled musician, poet, and philosopher. The nine met frequently with the Emperor to fulfill Akbar's great ideals. They became known as the Navratna—the nine jewels of the empire. Even Akbar's chefs were inspired—the recipe for this dish was created then and has come down doubtless unaltered in the time-honored way—by word of mouth.

Use nine vegetables of your choice, and the net weight after preparing should be 1 1/2 pounds. Choose vegetables that give good contrasting colors and which can be given approximately the same shape when cut. The following is my selection of nine.

INGREDIENTS

1 1/2 pounds vegetables: carrot, potato, rutabaga, parsnip, daikon (white radish), peas, beans, yellow and red bell peppers

3 tablespoons vegetable oil

20 almonds

1 teaspoon Garlic Purée (see page 16)

1 teaspoon Ginger Purée (see page 16)

8 tablespoons Onion Purée (see page 17)

1–4 fresh green hot peppers, chopped (to taste, optional)

1 tablespoon chopped fresh cilantro leaves

1 1/4 cups milk

Akhni Stock (see page 23) or water

1 tablespoon golden raisins (optional)

2 teaspoons Garam Masala (storebought or homemade, see page 35)

1 teaspoon saffron

14 tablespoons light cream

1 teaspoon sugar (optional)

Salt to taste

SPICES

1/4 teaspoon fennel seeds

1/2 teaspoon black cumin seeds

1 teaspoon green cardamoms

2-inch piece cassia bark or cinnamon stick

METHOD

■ Prepare the vegetables. Blanch the first five, then dice them into 1/2-inch cubes. Slice the beans to the same length, and the peppers into diamond shapes.

■ Heat the oil in a *karahi* or wok, and fry the almonds for 2 minutes. Drain the almonds well and set aside. Using the same oil, stir-fry the **Spices** for 1 minute, then the garlic purée for 1 minute, the ginger purée for 1 minute, and the onion purée for 5 minutes. Add the hot peppers, if using, and fresh cilantro.

■ Add all the vegetables and the milk, and simmer for 5 minutes. Add stock or water if you want a runnier consistency.

■ Add the golden raisins, fried almonds, garam masala, saffron, cream, sugar, and salt to taste. When simmering it is ready to serve. It should be nice and creamy and very colorful, and it goes well with a dry dish such as stuffed quail, accompanied by *naan* or stuffed eggplant and rice.

Niramish

STIR-FRIED MIXED VEGETABLES

SERVES 4
AS A MAIN
COURSE

A Bengali recipe devised, it is said, for newly widowed Hindu women, *niramish* is also called *shukto niramis Turkari*. The recipe contains no onion and very little spicing, which it is supposed will keep the widows' sexual appetites down! Cooked in mustard oil with panch phoran and lemon juice, the mix of lightly cooked vegetables gives a nutty taste.

Use your own choice of vegetables in season. Simply blanch them, then stir-fry with subtle spices and herbs to produce a crispy crunchy side or main dish, full of vitamins and health, giving nutrients as well as taste.

INGREDIENTS

1 1/2 pounds vegetables: any four of okra, green beans, cauliflower, summer squash, carrot, potatoes, peas	**SPICES**
	2 teaspoons *Panch Phoran* (see page 36)
	1/2 teaspoon turmeric
6 tablespoons mustard or peanut oil	1/2–2 teaspoons ground red pepper (cayenne)
Juice of 1 lemon	
1 tablespoon chopped fresh cilantro leaves	
Salt to taste	

119

METHOD

■ Prepare the vegetables, and blanch those that need it. If using okra, prepare as on pages 114–115.

■ Heat the oil, and fry the **Spices** for 1 minute. Stir-fry the okra first, if being used, for 2 minutes. Then add the other vegetables. Stir-fry for 7–8 more minutes.

■ Then add the lemon juice, fresh cilantro, and salt to taste. Toss for 2–3 more minutes. Serve fresh. Will keep or freeze, but this is not ideal—the crisp texture is lost.

Sabzi Dilruba

VEGETABLES IN A CREAMY SAUCE

SERVES 4
AS A MAIN
COURSE

This is a choice of vegetables cooked with crumbled *paneer*, eggs, and nuts in a creamy sauce. The dish can trace its roots directly to Iran (where *sabzi* also means vegetables), containing a typical Persian combination of flavors and textures.

INGREDIENTS

1 1/2 pounds vegetables, made up as follows:
    1 medium-size zucchini (about 1 pound)
    4 ounces each of peas and green beans

2 tablespoons vegetable oil

8 tablespoons Curry Masala Sauce (see page 22)

2 tomatoes, quartered

1 recipe Paneer (see page 33), crumbled

3 tablespoons peanuts

6–8 whole quail eggs, hard-boiled for 4 minutes, or 2 chicken eggs, hard-boiled and chopped

1/4 cup light cream

Water

Salt to taste

SPICES

1/2 teaspoon turmeric

1 teaspoon ground cumin

1 teaspoon ground coriander

1/4 teaspoon fenugreek seeds

1/4 teaspoon asafoetida

METHOD

■ Peel the zucchini and cut into cubes. To blanch it, place in a strainer over a pan of boiling water, with the lid on the strainer, so the zucchini is not immersed, then steam for 5–7 minutes.

■ Heat the oil. Stir-fry the **Spices** for 1 minute, then add the curry sauce and fry for another 5 minutes.

■ Add the tomato, peas, and beans and simmer for 3 minutes. Add the crumbled paneer, peanuts, whole or chopped eggs, zucchini, and cream. Add a little water if you require it, and some salt to taste. Serve when simmering.

Kayla Foogath

BANANA CURRY

SERVES 4
GENEROUSLY
AS A SIDE

A *foogath* is a particular method of vegetable cooking in the south of India, particularly in the Malabar areas. The principal vegetable in this case is *kayla* or banana and providing you don't overcook it, it is superb. But you can *foogath* any vegetable or combination. Note the near absence of spicing.

INGREDIENTS

2 tablespoons ghee or mustard oil (or walnut oil)	1/2 green bell pepper, seeded and sliced
4 bananas, peeled and chopped	1 tomato, chopped
Juice of 1 lemon	Salt to taste
	Ground red pepper (cayenne)

METHOD

■ Heat the oil and add the bananas, followed by the other ingredients.

■ Heat up to the sizzling stage, gently toss, and serve immediately.

Avial

MALABAR MIXED VEGETABLES

SERVES 4
GENEROUSLY
AS A MAIN
COURSE

Avial is known as the Malabar masterpiece. It is traditionally made from a combination of yogurt and vegetables and does not use tamarind and *dhal* (they are less available there). Traditionally the dish would contain a combination of some of the following: eggplant, plantain, yam, pumpkin, bitter and ash gourd. Also used are potato, stalks of spinach or broccoli, cucumber, and carrot. Mandatory is green (sour) mango, yogurt, and coconut.

Avial is prepared on certain occasions at the great temples of the south for mass feedings in vast brass urns, five feet high and ten feet in diameter, and is a tradition which goes back to the Chola temple builders of the tenth century.

INGREDIENTS

1 1/2 pounds mixed vegetables	1 small sour mango, skinned, pitted, and chopped (or 1 teaspoon mango powder)
Flesh of 1/2 a fresh coconut and its water, or 2 tablespoons flaked coconut, mixed to a paste with water	1/4 cup plain yogurt
	10 curry leaves
2–4 fresh green hot peppers, roughly chopped (to taste)	Salt to taste
2 teaspoons cumin seeds	4 tablespoons coconut oil
1 teaspoon turmeric	Coconut ground to a powder, if required

METHOD

■ Prepare and trim the vegetables, as appropriate. The tradition is to cut them into thin diamond-shaped slices.

■ Make a paste in a blender or food processor of the coconut, peppers, cumin seeds, and turmeric with the coconut water. Add a little water if necessary.

■ Blanch the vegetables for 3–4 minutes in plenty of water, then strain, reserving enough blanching water to cover the vegetables in a pan.

■ Add the mango flesh, yogurt, curry leaves, and the paste. Simmer for a short while until the vegetables are ready. Add salt to taste.

■ Just before serving, heat and add the coconut oil. If it is very watery, add some coconut powder to thicken it.

Bundghobi Poriyal

SOUTH INDIAN SHREDDED CABBAGE

SERVES 4
GENEROUSLY
AS A SIDE

INGREDIENTS

1 green cabbage, about 1 1/2 pounds in weight, shredded in a food processor	1 tablespoon chopped fresh cilantro leaves
4 tablespoons coconut oil, mustard oil, or peanut oil	Flesh of 1 coconut, shredded, and its water
1 teaspoon mustard seeds	Salt to taste
1 large Spanish onion, peeled and finely chopped	

METHOD

■ Blanch the shredded cabbage in boiling water for 1–2 minutes, then drain.

■ Heat the oil and fry the mustard seeds for 2 minutes, the onion for 3 minutes, then the fresh cilantro for 1 minute.

■ Place the cabbage in the pan and stir-fry until hot. Use the coconut water to keep it moist. Add the shredded coconut. Salt to taste and serve. Garnish, if you like, with some steamed white lentils (*urid dhal*) and fresh cilantro.

Bhare Mirchi

STUFFED PEPPER CURRY

**SERVES 4
AS A MAIN
COURSE**

Whole green peppers stuffed with spicy mashed potatoes and braised in a curry sauce, this makes a delicious vegetarian main course, served with Indian bread.

There are many vegetables that offer themselves as candidates for stuffing, including potatoes, bell peppers, tomatoes, mushrooms (fiddly but nice), zucchini, and eggplant (see next recipe). I've even come across apples and mangoes scooped out and stuffed with curry. Use your imagination!

INGREDIENTS

4 medium to large firm green or red bell peppers

POTATO FILLING

2 large potatoes, about 12 ounces in total, peeled

1 medium onion, peeled and chopped

2 fresh green hot peppers, chopped

1/2 teaspoon Garam Masala (storebought or homemade, see page 35)

Salt

SAUCE

1 medium onion, peeled and finely chopped

2 garlic cloves, finely chopped

1-inch piece fresh ginger

Vegetable oil

1 1/4 cups stock or tomato juice

Salt

SAUCE SPICES

1 teaspoon each of turmeric, cumin seeds, Garam Masala (storebought or homemade, see page 35)

1-2 teaspoons water

METHOD

■ To prepare the peppers, cut the stalk end off, leaving a hole of 2 inches diameter. Carefully remove the pithy center and seeds.

■ Blanch for 2 minutes in boiling water. Set aside.

■ For the potato filling, boil the potatoes, then mash them.

■ Add the onion, hot peppers, and garam masala, with salt to taste.

■ For the sauce, fry the onion, garlic, and ginger in some oil until golden (about 15 minutes).

■ Make a paste of the **Sauce spices** with a little water, then add to the fried mixture.

- Fry for 5–10 minutes, stirring frequently, then add stock or tomato juice and some salt. Simmer until needed.

- Fill each pepper with the cooked potato filling, and place in an oven dish that enables the peppers to stand upright without falling over.

- Gently pour the sauce into the oven dish and cook for 15–20 minutes in an oven preheated to 325°F.

Stuffed Baby Eggplant

SERVES 4
AS A SIDE

The art of all vegetable cooking is to produce a dish that is not overcooked or mushy, but timed to crispy perfection. It is much harder to do this with vegetables than with meat, particularly in the busy kitchen.

INGREDIENTS

8 small eggplant, about 2–3 ounces each

STUFFING

2 tablespoons vegetable oil

1/4 Spanish onion, peeled and finely chopped

1–4 green hot peppers, finely chopped (to taste)

4 tablespoons frozen peas

1 tablespoon chopped fresh cilantro leaves

1 tablespoon freshly grated or flaked coconut

1 tablespoon raw cashew nuts, chopped

1 tablespoon raisins, chopped (optional)

Salt to taste

SPICES

1 teaspoon ground coriander

1 teaspoon cumin seeds, roasted

1 teaspoon Garam Masala (storebought or homemade, see page 35)

1/4 teaspoon asafoetida

METHOD

- Make the stuffing first, allowing it to cool, at least enough to handle. Heat the oil and stir-fry the onion for 2 minutes. Add the **Spices** and stir-fry for another 2 minutes.

- Add all the remaining ingredients, mix well, and cook for another 2 minutes, creating a dry mixture. Remove from heat and leave to cool. (This quantity is generous—if you have extra stuffing, freeze for future use in any curry base.)

■ When ready for the final stage, boil some water. Wash the eggplant, and blanch them for 3 minutes.

■ Cut off the stalk and slit each eggplant to create a pocket. Carefully stuff the pocket with the filling. Place the filled eggplant in an oven tray and into a preheated 325°F oven for about 15 minutes. Serve immediately—the dish does not keep or freeze, it becomes mushy. If you want to serve a sauce with it, a delicious sauce is *kudhi* (page 38).

Paneer Korma

SERVES 4
AS A SIDE

In this recipe, *paneer* is compressed, cut into cubes, then deep-fried. The cubes have very little taste, but combined with a creamy sauce make a delicious curry.

INGREDIENTS

4 tablespoons ghee	**SPICES 1 (GROUND)**
1-inch cube fresh ginger, cut into julienne	1 teaspoon cumin
1 Spanish onion, peeled and thinly sliced	1 teaspoon turmeric
About 1/3 cup plain yogurt	1 teaspoon coriander
2 tablespoons chickpea flour (*besan*)	1 teaspoon garlic powder
2 teaspoons brown sugar	1-3 teaspoons water
2 teaspoons tomato purée	**SPICES 2 (WHOLE)**
1 1/4 cups *paneer* whey (see page 33)	12 green cardamoms
Salt to taste	4 cloves
1 recipe *Paneer* Cheese (see page 33)	1 teaspoon white cumin seeds
20 strands saffron	1/2 teaspoon black cumin seeds
1 tablespoon chopped fresh cilantro leaves	1/2 teaspoon fennel seeds or aniseed
	2 star anises

METHOD

■ Make a paste of **Spices 1** with a little water. Heat the ghee and stir-fry **Spices 2** for 1 minute, the ginger for 2 minutes, and the onion for 5 minutes. Now add the spice paste, and stir-fry for 3 more minutes.

■ Add the yogurt and the chickpea flour, sugar, and tomato purée. Stir in well, then add the whey. Salt to taste and add the paneer. When simmering, add the saffron and cilantro. Serve after 2 more minutes.

Malai Kofta

VEGETABLE BALLS IN CREAM SAUCE

SERVES 4 AS MAIN COURSE

*K*ofta means round or ball shaped. This *kofta* uses mashed potato as the main ingredient of the balls. These are deep-fried, then, just before serving, simmered in a curry sauce containing cream (*malai*). Zucchini or other squash are most commonly used for this dish and are extremely popular in India (grate and bind with mashed potato and chickpea flour), but you could use any vegetable that shreds easily. Koftas need to be served freshly made.

INGREDIENTS

KOFTAS

2 cups mashed potato

1 tablespoon raisins

2 tablespoons cashew nuts, ground

1 tablespoon curry powder

1/2 teaspoon salt

1 teaspoon sugar

SAUCE

4 tablespoons mustard or peanut oil

1 tablespoon Curry Paste (storebought or homemade, see page 20)

2 teaspoons Garlic Purée (see page 16)

2 teaspoons Ginger Purée (see page 16)

8 tablespoons Onion Purée (see page 17)

2/3 cup Akhni Stock (see page 23) or water

1 teaspoon tomato purée

6 tablespoons vegetable oil

4 ounces Paneer Cheese (see page 33) cut into 1/4-inch cubes

12 whole cashew nuts

GARNISH

1 tablespoon whipping cream

METHOD

■ To make the *koftas*, mix together all the ingredients. The mixture should be glutinous enough to form into balls. Set aside.

■ For the sauce, heat the mustard oil in a pan and stir-fry the curry paste for 1 minute, then the garlic purée for 1 minute, the ginger purée for 1 minute, and the onion purée for 5 minutes. Add the stock or water and tomato purée and simmer.

■ Heat the vegetable oil in a *karahi* or wok, and stir-fry the *paneer* and nuts together until both are golden (it only takes a couple of minutes, so it is worth concentrating). Strain well, and put the *paneer* and nuts into the sauce. Keep warm.

■ Heat the same oil in the *karahi*, and very carefully fry the *koftas* until they are hot throughout and golden in color (about 4–5 minutes).

■ To serve, place the balls in a serving dish. Put the warm sauce over them and garnish with the cream.

Bombay Potato

SERVES 4
AS A SIDE

Potatoes—especially new ones—are excellent curry subjects. This is a simple dish: potatoes boiled, then simmered in a curry sauce.

INGREDIENTS

4 tablespoons vegetable oil	SPICES
8 tablespoons Curry Masala Sauce (see page 22)	2 teaspoons Garam Masala (storebought or homemade, see page 35)
2 tomatoes, roughly chopped	1 teaspoon turmeric
1 1/2 pounds new potatoes (or large, older ones, quartered), cooked	1/2–2 teaspoons ground red pepper (cayenne)
Salt to taste	1/2 teaspoon mango powder

METHOD

■ Heat the oil, and stir-fry the **Spices** for 30 seconds, then add the curry sauce. Stir-fry to 2 minutes, then add the tomatoes and simmer for 5 more minutes.

■ Now add the cooked potato, and simmer until hot. Salt to taste.

Aloo Podimas

SOUTH INDIAN POTATO

SERVES 4
AS A MAIN
COURSE

On long journeys on Indian Railways, your food is ordered and paid for at a stop en-route, then delivered to your carriage piping-hot at the next stop for you to eat as the train pulls on. The dirty dishes are collected at the next (third) stop. This potato dish was one that I had in this way on a train journey in Southern India. The system seems to be very complex, but it works right down to the last detail—the waiter even had the meal in his hands and was standing on the platform in exactly the right place to enter my carriage when the train stopped.

INGREDIENTS

1 1/2 pounds potato, peeled and diced	**SPICES**
2 teaspoons turmeric	2 teaspoons mustard seeds
6 tablespoons mustard or peanut oil	8 dry curry leaves
1 tablespoon *urid dhal*, crushed	1–6 dry red hot peppers (to taste)
1 Spanish onion, peeled and thinly sliced	1 teaspoon paprika
3 tomatoes, chopped	
Salt to taste	

METHOD

■ Boil the potatoes with the turmeric until tender but firm.

■ Meanwhile, heat the oil in a *karahi* or wok, and fry the **Spices** and the *dhal* for 2 minutes.

■ Add the onion slices and fry until brown (around 5 minutes).

■ Add the tomatoes to the pan and simmer until cooked (about 5 minutes).

■ Add the just-cooked potatoes, and toss well. Add salt to taste, then serve. This dish will keep chilled for a day. Freezing spoils the texture of the potato.

129

Aloo Makhanwalla

POTATO IN TANDOORI SAUCE

SERVES 4
GENEROUSLY
AS A SIDE

INGREDIENTS

1 1/2 pounds small new potatoes, scrubbed

2 tablespoons Tandoori Marinade (see page 31)

2 tablespoons ghee

8 tablespoons Curry Masala Sauce (see page 22)

1 tablespoon Curry Paste (storebought or homemade, see page 20)

4–6 tomatoes, puréed

2 tablespoons tomato ketchup

1 tablespoon chopped fresh cilantro leaves

Salt to taste

3 tablespoons light cream

SPICES 1

2 teaspoons cumin seeds

2 teaspoons mustard seeds

SPICES 2

2 teaspoons Garam Masala (storebought or homemade, see page 35)

2 teaspoons dry fenugreek leaf

METHOD

■ Leave the skins on the potatoes, but scrape them a little to help the marinade adhere. Rub in the marinade, coating well. Leave to stand for up to 6 hours.

■ Preheat the oven to 325°F. Place the potatoes and marinade on a baking tray, and bake for 15–20 minutes (depending on potato size).

■ Meanwhile, heat the ghee and stir-fry **Spices 1** for 1 minute, then the curry sauce for 3 minutes, and the paste for 2 minutes. Add the tomatoes and simmer for 5 minutes.

■ Add the ketchup, cilantro, **Spices 2**, and salt to taste. Simmer for another 4 minutes.

■ As soon as the potatoes are baked, add them to the sauce, and bring back to a simmer. Add the cream, mix, and serve fresh and hot when tender.

Bhara Aloo

SPICY BAKED POTATOES

SERVES 4
AS A SIDE

Nowhere before have I encountered baked potato in traditional Indian cooking. This is probably because Indian cooking has evolved over the last six thousand years without ovens, apart from the very high-heat tandoor. However, the modern oven allows us to bring forward new ideas with old subjects. *Bhara Aloo* can be stuffed with all sorts of fillings. Try, for example, a kebab filling (page 45) or perhaps a chicken *tikka masala* filling (pages 93–94). There are endless curry fillings one could use, but try this version first.

INGREDIENTS

4 large potatoes, around 6 ounces each	1/4 cup whipping cream
2 tablespoons vegetable oil	Salt to taste
2 large scallions with green, trimmed and chopped	4 tablespoons grated cheddar cheese
1 teaspoon Garlic Purée (see page 16)	SPICES
1 teaspoon Ginger Purée (see page 16)	1 teaspoon cumin seeds, roasted
1/2 each red and green bell peppers, seeded and finely chopped	1 teaspoon ground red pepper (cayenne)
6 tablespoons cooked rice (leftovers are excellent)	1 teaspoon Mild Curry Powder (store-bought or homemade, see page 12)
	1 teaspoon Garam Masala (storebought or homemade, see page 35)

METHOD

■ Wash, scrub, and prick the potatoes, and wrap them in aluminum foil.

■ In the oven, preheated to 400°F, bake for about 1 hour. Test that they are cooked by poking with a thick cooking knife.

■ Meanwhile, make the stuffing. Heat the oil and stir-fry the scallions for 2 minutes, the garlic purée for 1 minute, the ginger purée for 1 minute, and the **Spices** for 1 minute. Add the bell peppers and stir-fry for another 3–4 minutes. Add the rice, cream, and salt. Toss to mix, then remove from the heat.

■ When the potatoes are cooked (keep them hot), remove the foil, and cut a small slice off the top of each, and scoop most of the potato out of the skin (keep for use in another recipe). Pack the stuffing into the pocket.

■ Sprinkle the grated cheese over the potatoes and broil to melt the cheese. Serve with any curry and Indian bread.

Kamal Kakri

LOTUS STEM CURRY

**SERVES 4
AS A SIDE**

This unusual dish comes from Kashmir, the northern-most state of India which nestles in the western Himalayan mountains. Eaten fresh, lotus roots have a taste and texture slightly resembling the fragrant Jerusalem artichoke. Being a rhizome, they transport well and can be found in Asian food stores from time to time. They are also available canned, but, not surprisingly, they are not as subtle in this form.

INGREDIENTS

1 pound lotus roots	**SPICES 1**
4 tablespoons vegetable oil	2 teaspoons cumin seeds
3 teaspoons Garlic Purée (see page 16)	**SPICES 2**
3 teaspoons Ginger Purée (see page 16)	1 teaspoon turmeric
1/2 Spanish onion, peeled and finely chopped	1 teaspoon ground red pepper (cayenne)
2 tomatoes, chopped	2 teaspoons Garam Masala (storebought or homemade, see page 35)
4 tablespoons chopped fresh cilantro leaves	
Salt to taste	

METHOD

■ Wash, scrape, and trim the lotus roots. Cut into small cubes, then boil in water until tender. Times vary according to the density of the particular root. If using canned, cube, wash, and set aside.

■ Heat the oil and add **Spices 1**. When they crackle, add the garlic and ginger purées, and stir-fry for 1 minute.

■ Add the onion and stir-fry until golden (about 5 minutes).

■ Add **Spices 2**, tomato, lotus, and cilantro leaves. Simmer for about 10 minutes, then salt to taste.

Tarka Chana Dhal

CHICKPEAS IN SPICY LENTIL PURÉE

**SERVES 4
AS A SIDE**

Like many people in southern India, I find *dhal* and plain rice not only filling and very tasty, but able to supply all the protein (from the lentils) and roughage (from the rice) that I need. I also enjoy chickpeas (*chana*). The idea of combining the two came to me one day and as far as I know it is an original recipe. It is easy to make, except that the *chana* requires a long soaking time. You can get around that by using canned or, as I do, by preparing a large batch of *chana* at a time. Simply boil it and, when cooked, cool under cold water, then strain and freeze. Before the chickpeas are rock hard, shake them around to separate them, so that, like peas, they are individually frozen and you can scoop out exactly the quantity you need. This dish freezes well too.

INGREDIENTS

1/2 cup dried *kabli chana* (chickpeas)	2 teaspoons Garlic Purée (see page 16)
1 3/4 cup Akhni Stock (see page 23) or water	6 tablespoons Onion Purée (see page 17)
1 1/2 cups dried *masoor dhal* (red lentils)	1 tablespoon Curry Paste (storebought or homemade, see page 20)
2 tablespoons ghee or vegetable oil	Salt to taste
2 teaspoons cumin seeds	

METHOD

■ Soak the chickpeas overnight to allow them to swell and soften. Strain and rinse well. Bring to a boil at least 5 cups water. Add the chickpeas and simmer for 45 minutes. Or you can use a can of chickpeas, adding them complete with their liquid to the cooked lentils.)

■ The lentils also need soaking, but only for an hour or so. Then strain and rinse. Boil 1 3/4 cups water (or stock for best taste). Add the lentils and cook for 30 minutes, stirring from time to time. The water should absorb into the lentils to produce a creamy purée.

■ Meanwhile, heat the oil and fry the cumin, then the garlic and the onion purée for 1 minute each.

■ When the lentils are cooked, add the onion mixture and the chickpeas, and heat. When hot, add the curry paste and mix in well. Taste and salt as needed. This dish is better cooked in advance—it will keep warm for ages—or it can be reheated. Make a larger quantity for freezing.

133

RICE AND BREAD

▲▲▲▲▲▲▲▲▲▲▲▲▲▲▲▲

The seeds of certain grasses such as barley, corn, millet, oats, rye, wheat, and rice have become essential or staple foods. Rice is the best-known partner to curry, but not all the peoples of India regard rice as their staple.

Wheat is used to make bread, which is eaten instead of rice as an accompaniment to curry.

Rice needs a combination of fresh water and humidity to succeed in widespread cultivation. It requires careful irrigation and thrives along the fertile areas on either side of rivers. Rice grows in many regions of India, especially in the foothills of the Himalayas, in the basins of the great rivers—and all around the southern coastal tributary areas. Rice is virtually the sole staple food in Bangladesh, Burma, Thailand, Malaysia, and Indonesia.

There are thousands of species of rice, but the one name that matters in curry cooking is basmati. It is a long-grained rice that when cooked has outstanding fragrance and texture.

Wheat grows in the hardier, drier parts of India, where rice does not grow. It thrives in central and north-western India, Nepal, Pakistan, Afghanistan, and all lands west, and does not grow in any of the curry lands to the east. The wheat-eating areas of India include Hyderabad, Lucknow, the Punjab, and Gujerat.

The breads of the sub-continent use a hard, finely milled whole-grain flour called *ata*, or *chupatti* flour.

Plain Boiled Rice

SERVES 4

This is the quickest way to cook rice, and it can be ready to serve just 15 minutes after the water boils. Two factors are crucial for this method to work perfectly. First, the rice must be basmati rice. *Patna* or long-grained, quick-cook, or other rices, will require different timings and will have neither the texture nor the fragrance of basmati. Second, it is one of the few recipes in this book that requires *precision timing*. It is essential that for its few minutes on the stove, you concentrate on it or else it may overcook and become soggy.

A 2/3-cup portion of dry rice provides an ample helping per person: 6 tablespoons will be a smaller but adequate portion. To spice the plain cooked rice, see the next two recipes.

INGREDIENTS

| 1 1/3–2 cups basmati or other long-grained rice | 2 2/3–4 cups water |

METHOD

- Pick through the rice to remove grit and particles.

- Boil the water. It is not necessary to salt it.

- While it is heating up, rinse the rice briskly with fresh cold water until most of the starch is washed out. Run hot tap water through the rice at the final rinse. This minimizes the temperature reduction of the boiling water when you put the rice into it.

- When the water is boiling properly, put the rice into the pan. Start timing. Put the lid on the pan until the water comes back to a boil, then remove.

- It takes 8–10 minutes from the start. Stir frequently.

- After about 6 minutes, taste a few grains. As soon as the center is no longer brittle, but still has a good *al dente* bite to it, strain off the water. It should seem slightly *under*cooked.

■ Shake off all excess water, then place the strainer onto a dry kitchen towel, which will help remove the last of the water.

■ After a minute, place the rice in a pre-warmed serving dish. You can serve it now or put it into a low oven or warming drawer for about half an hour minimum. As it dries, the grains will separate and become fluffy. It can be held in the warmer for several hours if needed.

Spiced Rice

SERVES 4

METHOD

■ For even tastier rice you can add ground coconut and ground almonds as on page 137.

■ You can also spice it as for the lemon rice method in the recipe on page 137.

■ If you want to achieve the different colored grains that restaurants do, you have to use food coloring powder (see below). The best color is sunset yellow, and to achieve it, simply sprinkle a tiny tip of the teaspoonful on top of the rice *before* it goes into the warmer. Do not stir it in. Allow it 30 minutes to soak in and *then* stir. You'll get a mixture of colored grains from deep to pale yellow mixed in with white. If you wish to go multicolored, with yellow, red and/or green, separate the rice into three portions, color as stated, and keep separate in warmer. Mix together after half an hour.

Quick Pullao Rice

SERVES 4

This and the following recipe are spicings for plain boiled rice which each only take 5 minutes—so you can be ready with a perfect *pullao* or lemon rice in as little as 20 minutes from the start.

INGREDIENTS

2 teaspoons ghee	Pinch sunset yellow food coloring (optional)
1 recipe Plain Boiled Rice (see page 135)	SPICES
2 teaspoons coconut ground to a powder	1 teaspoon fennel seeds
2 teaspoons ground almonds	1 teaspoon black cumin seeds

METHOD

- Heat the ghee and stir-fry the **Spices** for 30 seconds.

- Add the other ingredients, and stir in until hot.

- Serve immediately.

Quick Lemon Rice

SERVES 4

INGREDIENTS

2 teaspoons mustard or peanut oil	SPICES
1 recipe Plain Boiled Rice (see page 135)	1 teaspoon mustard seeds
2 tablespoons fried cashew nuts	1 teaspoon sesame seeds
1 teaspoon coconut, ground to a powder	1 teaspoon turmeric
Juice of 2 lemons	6 curry leaves, fresh or dry

METHOD

- Cook exactly as in the previous recipe.

Rice by Absorption

Cooking rice by a pre-measured ratio of rice to water which is all absorbed into the rice is undoubtedly the best way to do it. Provided that you use basmati rice, the finished grains are longer, thinner, and much more fragrant and flavorful than they are after boiling.

The method is easy, but many cookbooks make it sound far too complicated. Instructions invariably state that you must use a tightly lidded pot and precise water quantity and heat levels, and never lift the lid during the boiling process, etc., etc. However, I lift the lid, I might stir the rice, and I've even cooked rice by absorption *without* a lid. Also, if I've erred on the side of too little water, I've added a bit during boiling. (Too much water *is* an unresolvable problem.) It's all naughty, rule-breaking stuff, but it still seems to work.

Another factor, always omitted in other people's books, is the time factor. They all say or imply that rice must be served as soon as it is done. This causes stress to the cook who believes that there is no margin of error in time and method. In reality, the longer you give the rice to absorb the water/steam, the fluffier and more fragrant it will be. So it can be cooked well in advance of being required for serving. For after the initial boil and 10-minute simmer, the rice is quite sticky, and it needs to relax. After 30 minutes, it can be served and is fluffy, but it can be kept in a warm place for much longer—improving in fluffiness all the time. This is the way the restaurants do it. They cook in bulk using up to 9 pounds rice (around 60 portions) at a time in huge aluminum saucepans. They follow this recipe exactly (the timings do no change, no matter how much rice is being used). They cook their rice at the end of the lunch session, put it in a very low-heat oven, and by the opening of business at 6 PM it's perfect and, kept warm in the oven, lasts the whole evening.

Cooking rice does need practice. You may need one or two tries at it. Here are some tips for the newcomer.

■ Choose a pan, preferably with a lid, which can be used both on the stove and in the oven. Until you have had lots of practice, always use the same pan, so that you become familiar with it.

■ Keep a good eye on the clock. The timing is important or you'll burn the bottom of the rice. Use basmati rice.

■ If you intend to let the rice cool down for serving later, or the next day, or to freeze it, do not put it in the warmer. It is better slightly undercooked for these purposes.

After a few tries at this you'll do it without thinking. Here is my foolproof method. The full complement of spices listed below gives a really tasty rice. You can omit some if you don't have them on hand. Some restaurants just use the fennel and black cumin seeds and these are very fragrant. If you don't like chewy spices, omit or remove the cloves, bay, cassia, etc.

SERVES 4

INGREDIENTS

1 1/3 cups dry rice	2-inch piece cassia bark or cinnamon stick
2 1/2 cups water, *or*, for tastier results (the way restaurants do it), 1 1/4 cups milk, plus 1 1/4 cups water	2 bay leaves
1 tablespoon ghee	1 teaspoon fennel seeds
SPICES	1/2 teaspoon black cumin seeds
4 green cardamoms	1 brown cardamom
4 cloves	2 star anises

METHOD

- Soak the rice in water for about half an hour.

- Rinse it until the rinse water is more or less clear, then strain.

- Boil the water (or water and milk).

- In a saucepan (as heavy as possible, and with a lid), or a casserole dish at least twice the volume of the strained rice, heat the ghee, then fry the **Spices** for 30 seconds.

- Add the rice and stir-fry, ensuring the oil coats the rice, and it heats up.

- Then add the boiled water (or water and milk), and stir in well. Put the lid on, keep the heat high and cook for 8 minutes.

- Inspect. Has the liquid absorbed on top? If not, replace the lid and leave for 2 more minutes. If and when it has, stir the rice well, ensuring that it is not sticking to the bottom. Now taste. It should not be brittle in the middle. If it is, add a little more water and keep on high heat a little longer.

- Place the saucepan or casserole into an oven preheated to its very lowest setting. The longer you leave the rice, the more separate the grains will be. An hour is fine, but it will be quite safe and happy left for several hours.

Quick-Style Biriani/Pullao

SERVES 4

This quick *biriani* and *pullao* consists of pre-cooked meat, chicken, shrimp, or vegetable, dry-fried with a little curry sauce into which pre-cooked *pullao* rice is stir-fried. *Pullao* is served at this point in the preparation. *Biriani* sometimes has a separate onion and whole spice *tarka* stir-fried in or applied as a garnish along with fried egg, almonds, tomato, and golden raisins; it is normally served with curry sauce (a combination of a quick fry-up of some spices and Curry Masala Sauce as on page 22).

These methods work passably well, but the traditional methods of making *pullaos* and *birianis* in the following recipes are worth trying. You'll capture the maximum flavors by using the absorption techniques.

INGREDIENTS

1 tablespoon ghee or oil	**GARNISHES**
6 tablespoons sliced onion	Fried onion
1 teaspoon Curry Paste (storebought or homemade, see page 20)	Fried egg or omelet
	Whole fried almonds
2 tablespoons Curry Masala Sauce (see page 22)	Fresh tomato slices
2 cups pre-cooked meat	Golden raisins
2 1/4 cups pre-cooked *Pullao* Rice (see page 137)	Flaked coconut

METHOD

■ Heat the oil and stir-fry the onion until golden brown (5–8 minutes). Remove half for garnish.

■ Add the curry paste to the onion in the pan and fry for 1 minute, then add the curry masala sauce. Heat until simmering, then add the meat, which should soak up the sauce. When it does, add the rice. Mix well—but gently.

■ Serve hot, accompanied by garnishes.

Akhni Pullao

SPICY RICE WITH CHICKPEAS

SERVES 4

INGREDIENTS

1–1 1/2 cups uncooked basmati rice	
2 tablespoons ghee	
1-inch piece fresh ginger, sliced	
1/2 Spanish onion, peeled and chopped	
1/4 green bell pepper, seeded and sliced	
2–4 fresh green hot peppers, chopped (to taste)	
1 tablespoon chopped fresh cilantro leaves	
1/4 cup chickpeas, cooked	
Salt to taste	

SPICES

4 green cardamoms

4 cloves

2-inch piece cassia bark or cinnamon stick

2 bay leaves

1/2 teaspoon turmeric

GARNISH

8–10 pistachio nuts, sliced

METHOD

■ Soak the rice for 30 minutes, then rinse.

■ Warm a lidded casserole and heat the ghee. Stir-fry the ginger for 1 minute, then the onions for 3 minutes. Add the sweet and hot peppers and **Spices**. Cook for 3 minutes, and when soft, add the cilantro and chickpeas.

■ Stir in the rice. Add boiling water to cover the rice by about one-third of its depth, and bring to a boil. When the rice rises, cover the pot, turn down to simmer, and leave alone until the water has been absorbed by the rice (about 10 minutes).

■ Place the pot in a preheated oven at its lowest heat for at least 30 minutes.

■ After this, remove the rice and stir it with a fork to fluff it and let the steam escape. Serve with a garnish of pistachio nuts.

Kedgeree

RICE WITH LENTILS

SERVES 4

The British in India produced a unique range of dishes, Anglo-Indian cuisine, now sadly becoming gradually forgotten. Many of these dishes were adaptations of long-established Indian dishes, and one of these, which still remains in both forms is kedgeree or *kitchri*. The former is the Anglo-Indian version of a rice dish, a sort of *pullao* that contains smoked haddock, boiled egg, and pepper. The original Indian dish is Gujerati in origin and is a mixture of rice and lentils.

INGREDIENTS

1–1 1/2 cups uncooked basmati rice	**SPICES**
2 tablespoons ghee	1 teaspoon white cumin seeds
1 teaspoon Garlic Purée (see page 16)	1 teaspoon black mustard seeds
1/2 Spanish onion, peeled and thinly sliced	
1/2 cup *masoor dhal* (red lentils)	

METHOD

■ Soak the rice for 30 minutes, then rinse

■ Heat the ghee, and stir-fry the **Spices**, garlic purée, and onion for 5 minutes.

■ Boil the lentils in water (page 86). Do so completely, until they are soft, if adding to boiled rice; cook only halfway if adding to rice cooked by the absorption method.

■ If boiling the rice, add the fried items and the lentils after it has been strained, mixing it well.

■ If cooking the rice by absorption, add it to the ghee-fried ingredients, along with the half-cooked lentils, and proceed as on pages 138–139.

Navrattan Pullao

SERVES 4

This rice dish has a combination of nine vegetables, fruits, and nuts. You can cut down on the number of ingredients, or you can add more or alternatives. It is a very festive and decorative dish with wide appeal. The edible silver (or gold) leaf garnish makes an interesting conversation piece (page 144).

INGREDIENTS

1–1/2 cups uncooked basmati rice	1 tablespoon *chirongee* seeds
6 tablespoons ghee	1/2 teaspoon salt
8 small cauliflower florets, blanched	SPICES
1–2 carrots, diced and blanched	3 cloves
1 zucchini, diced and blanched	2 green cardamoms
2 tablespoons green peas, blanched	1/8 teaspoon ground mace
1 tablespoon grapes, seedless preferably	GARNISHES
1 slice pineapple, diced	Rosewater
1/2 apple, diced	4 sheets silver leaf (*vark*) (see page 144)
1 tablespoon cashew nuts	
1 tablespoon almonds	

METHOD

- Soak the rice for 30 minutes, then rinse well.

- Heat the ghee, and stir-fry the **Spices** for 1 minute.

- If boiling the rice, add the spices, vegetables, and other ingredients after it has been strained, mixing in well. Place in the oven for a short while.

- If cooking the rice by absorption, add the rice to the **Spices** and cook as on pages 138–139. Mix in the vegetables and other ingredients once it is cooked and then place in the oven.

- Sprinkle just before serving with the rosewater, and garnish with the *vark*.

Noor Mahal Biriani

SERVES 4

This dish originated in the city of Lucknow. It is a rich and colorful dish—a meal in itself—and is typical of the good-living days of Lucknow in the early nineteenth century.

The colors are achieved by coloring the cashew nuts, and the edible silver and/or gold leaf ornaments (*vark*) are said to have been created by the chefs of the happy-go-lucky Nawabs, the rulers of the day, to reflect the colors of the local attire. To this day, the saris of the area are more often than not traditionally red, green, or yellow with an immense amount of gold or silver filigree work on them.

The tradition of garnishing biriani dishes, as well as fudge-like sweets (*barfi*), goes back inevitably to the Moghul emperors. They took great delight in displaying their wealth, and eating it. At certain banquets, it is said, rice dishes contained pearls and cloves made from solid gold, which the recipient was supposed to return to the emperor with due thanks upon finding it in his serving. Rumor has it that certain guests of the emperor knowingly swallowed these trinkets so as to be able to smuggle them out of the royal presence and recover them later. Be that as it may, the silver and gold leaf was for eating, and the tradition has been carried on to this day. I have seen silver leaf being made in a small workshop in Hyderabad. The craftsman takes a small nugget of silver, then places it in a leather pouch. He proceeds to beat the pouch with a special hammer until the silver is thinner than cigarette papers and about five-inches square. It is then placed between sheets of tissue paper (this craftsman was using old railway timetables) and sold in lots of 100.

To use, carefully peel off the outer piece of tissue paper and discard, ensuring the silver or gold leaf has not stuck to it. Then lift up the next sheet of tissue and dab the leaf onto the hot food. Do not finger it, or it will disintegrate. Supplies are very hard to obtain in the West, and I have been advised by health officials that it is common practice to adulterate the silver with aluminum.

One final word about *vark*…it is said that it is an aphrodisiac. It is not for me to confirm or deny this, but it will certain make an interesting conversation piece if you use it for your next party!

INGREDIENTS

1–1 1/2 cups uncooked basmati rice	Akhni Stock (see page 23) or water
4 ounces ground lamb or beef	SPICES (ROASTED AND GROUND)
Salt to taste	4-inch piece cassia bark or cinnamon stick
1 teaspoon Garam Masala (storebought or homemade, see page 35)	1/2 nutmeg
3 tablespoons Garlic Purée (see page 16)	6 cloves
6 tablespoons ghee	6 green cardamom
8 tablespoons Onion Purée (see page 17)	GARNISHES
2 teaspoons Ginger Purée (see page 16)	6 tablespoons raw cashew nuts
2 ounces lean lamb or beef, cubed	Red, green, and yellow food coloring (optional)
1/3 cup plain yogurt	Some fresh red cherries (or bottled Maraschinos)
3/4 to 1 cup water	4 sheets of silver leak (*vark*) (see page 144)
Salt to taste	
1/2 teaspoon paprika	
1/2 teaspoon ground black pepper	

METHOD

■ Wash the rice well and soak in cold water for 30 minutes, then drain.

■ Mix the ground lamb with some salt, the garam masala, and 1 teaspoon of the garlic purée until blended well. Form into small *koftas* (balls).

■ Heat the ghee in a large, heavy saucepan and fry the onion purée, remaining garlic purée, and the ginger purée until golden. Add the cubes of lamb and fry, stirring, until the color changes.

■ Stir in the yogurt mixed with 3/4 to 1 cup water, some salt, the paprika, and pepper. Cover and cook until the lamb is half done (about 15 minutes).

■ Now add the *koftas*, and continue cooking until the lamb is tender, stirring occasionally. If there is too much liquid in the pan, uncover and cook, stirring, until it has almost all evaporated.

■ Now add the rice, the **Spices**, and enough stock or water to cover the rice by one-third. Bring to a boil, cover with a well-fitting lid, turn heat very low, and cook for 25 minutes without lifting the lid, until all the liquid has been absorbed. Uncover and allow steam to escape for a couple of minutes.

■ While the rice is cooking, boil the cashew-nut garnish separately in water to which some food coloring has been added (a few minutes). Color some cashews red, some green, and some yellow. Ground turmeric may be used for the yellow coloring or, if preferred, simply fry the nuts in oil until golden brown.

■ When the *biriani* is ready, garnish with nuts, cherries, and *vark*. Serve piping hot as a main dish in its own right—you won't really need another meat or veg dish—with sauce, bread, chutneys, and *pappadams*.

Naan Bread

MAKES 4

Naan is a huge, light, fluffy, and chewy flatbread, made from white flour lightly leavened and spiced. It's cooked traditionally by hanging in the tandoor, which accounts for the tear-drop shape, but in this recipe it's grilled.

INGREDIENTS

2 ounces fresh yeast, *or* 3 tablespoons plain yogurt	**SPICES**
	2 teaspoons sesame seeds
Lukewarm water	2 teaspoons wild onion seeds
6 cups white bread flour, *or* 3 cups white bread flour plus 3 cups white *chupatti* (ata) flour	
Melted ghee	

METHOD

■ Melt the fresh yeast in a little warm water until it has dissolved.

■ Put the flour in a warmed bowl, make a well in the center, and pour in the melted yeast or the yogurt.

■ Gently mix into the flour, and add enough warm water to make a firm dough

- Remove from the bowl and knead on a floured board until well combined. Return to the bowl and leave in a warm place for a couple of hours to rise.

- The dough, when risen, should double in size. It should be bubbly, stringy, and like elastic.

- Knock back the dough by kneading it down to its original size. Add the **Spices**.

- Divide the dough into four pieces and roll each into an oblong shape. The tear-drop shape comes from the dough being hung inside the tandoor, and if you want that shape, roll accordingly.

- Preheat the broiler to its maximum temperature. Place some foil on the broiler-pan rack to catch drips. Put the *naan* on the foil and the pan at the halfway rack. Brush one side of each naan with melted ghee and place under the broiler. Watch them cook (they can *over*cook and burn very easily). As the first side develops brown patches, remove and turn. Brush more ghee on the turned side and replace under the heat. Serve immediately.

Keema Naan

MINCE-STUFFED TANDOORI BREAD

MAKES 4

As with most Indian breads, the *naan* can be stuffed or folded around a filling. The filling is based on a traditional mince (*keema*), but in this case it is first tandoori-baked in a flat disk.

INGREDIENTS

Approx. 6 ounces raw Sheek Kebab (see page 45)	1 recipe *Naan* bread dough (see page 146)

METHOD

- Divide the kebab mix into four, and flatten each into a 4-inch oval disk.

- Either fry the disks on a *tava* or bake in the oven at 325°F for 10–15 minutes. Allow to cool.

- Make up the *naan* dough as in the previous recipe. Carefully enclose the kebab disk inside the dough and roll out. Proceed with the *naan* recipe as directed.

Onion Kulcha

LEAVENED WHITE BREAD

MAKES 4

This specialty bread from central India is made from the same dough as *naan* bread. The traditional shape is square with a decorative cross pattern made with the fingertips. This version has an onion stuffing.

INGREDIENTS

1 recipe *Naan* bread dough (see page 146) incorporating 4 cups flour and 2 tablespoons melted ghee	4 tablespoons sliced onions, fried in ghee until brown

METHOD

- Divide the dough into four balls

- Roll each out roughly and place equal amounts of cold onion in each. Fold the dough over the onion. Re-roll to a square of about 6 inches.

- Mark a cross shape, dotting with a finger, if you like, then bake as with *naan*.

Paratha

UNLEAVENED LAYERED WHEAT BREAD

MAKES 4

Parathas are the Indian version of layered bread (a sort of puff pastry). When pan-fried they should end up crispy on the outside yet meltingly soft.

INGREDIENTS

4 cups *ata or* whole-wheat flour	1 cup tepid water
Melted ghee	

METHOD

■ Mix the flour and 2 tablespoons of the ghee with enough tepid water to make a soft dough.

■ Divide the dough into four. Roll each piece into a long sausage, then flatten it into a strip about 12 x 3 inches. Apply melted ghee to the strip, then roll it up from the long side to make a snake. Coil the snake around itself into a shape like a three-dimensional ice-cream cone, narrow point up.

■ Sprinkle extra flour on the cone, then gently push it down with the hand and then roll it out to an 8-inch disk.

■ Heat 2 tablespoons ghee on a *tava* and fry the *paratha* until it is hot. Lift it out with tongs. Add more ghee and repeat on the other side.

Puri

DEEP-FRIED UNLEAVENED BREAD

MAKES 16

The *puri* uses the same *ata* flour dough as the *paratha*. Serve with the dishes of your choice. It goes particularly well with Shrimp Pathia on page 51.

INGREDIENTS

2 cups ata or whole-wheat flour	1/4 teaspoon salt
1 tablespoon ghee	Vegetable oil for deep-frying
3/4–1 cup hot water	

METHOD

■ Make a soft dough from the flour, ghee, water, and salt. Let it stand to soften and absorb fully for half an hour.

■ Divide into four, then divide each four into four—it's the easiest way of getting 16 similar-sized pieces.

■ Shape each into a ball, then roll out to 4-inch disks.

■ Preheat oil or a deep-fry to 375°F and immerse one disk in the oil at a time. It should puff up quickly. Turn when it does, and remove after 30 seconds. Serve at once.

Loochi

DEEP-FRIED UNLEAVENED WHITE BREAD

From the North-West Frontier, the *loochi* is a white flour version of the previous *puri* recipe. Simply make with 2 cups white bread flour in place of the *ata* or whole-wheat flour.

Bhatura

LEAVENED WHITE FLOUR AND SEMOLINA BREAD

MAKES 16

This Punjabi style of bread uses approximately two parts of white flour and one part of semolina (ground durum-wheat flour) to produce an interesting texture. Traditionally *bhatura* are eaten with *chana* (page 44), but they go nicely with everything.

INGREDIENTS

1 1/4 cups white bread flour	1/2 teaspoon salt
2/3 cup semolina	3/4 to 1 cup warm water
2 teaspoons plain yogurt	Vegetable oil for deep-frying

METHOD

■ Mix the flour, semolina, yogurt, and salt with enough warm water to make a dough as for *puri*.

■ Leave it to stand in a warm place to rise (about a couple of hours).

■ Roll out to 4-inch disks, and deep-fry in hot oil as for *puri* until golden. Shake off excess oil, and serve at once.

Makki-ki-Roti

RICE FLOUR BREAD

SERVES 4

Kashmir, high in the western Himalayas, is a rice-eating area, and wheat eating was, until very recent times, unknown. Rice flour is the Kashmiri alternative to wheat.

INGREDIENTS

8 ounces rice flour	1/4 to 1/2 cup water to make dough
1 teaspoon salt	Ghee
1/2 teaspoon ground red pepper (cayenne)	

METHOD

- Mix the rice flour, salt, and cayenne with enough water to make a soft dough. Let it stand for half an hour.

- Divide the dough into four, and roll each piece out to form a large disk about 8 inches in diameter.

- Dry-cook it on a tava or griddle. As it flecks to brown, turn over and do the same to the other side.

- Serve spread with ghee.

ACCOMPANIMENTS

▲▲▲▲▲▲▲▲▲▲▲▲▲▲▲▲▲▲▲

Indian food is a fabulous combination of rich creamy curries with fluffy rice or tasty breads, but it is the chutney and pickle dishes that are the perfect and indispensable accompaniment to the Indian meal. The tangy fresh salads in this chapter are very easy to make and are one of the few raw vegetable intakes (therefore containing vitamin C) in the Indian repertoire. Being tangy, they activate the salivary glands and improve the digestive process.

So, too, do bottled pickles, and there are dozens of very good varieties on the market. Most use lime, hot pepper, or mango, and they can vary enormously from very sour to very sweet (mango), and very mild to very hot.

Onion Salad

YIELDS ABOUT
1/2 CUP

The standard fresh chutney. Make this early so that the onion marinates and softens. Cover the bowl with plastic wrap and keep in the refrigerator.

INGREDIENTS

1/2 Spanish onion, peeled and thinly sliced	Pinch of dried mint
Juice of 1/2 lemon	

METHOD

- Simply mix all the ingredients together.

Indian Salad

SERVES 4
AS A SIDE

This delightful combination of flavor and color is served as a starter or accompaniment.

INGREDIENTS

8 walnuts, halved	1 cup bean sprouts
6 radishes, sliced	Juice of 2 lemons
1 tablespoon raisins	1 teaspoon dried mint
3-inch piece cucumber, sliced	Salt to taste

METHOD

- Simply mix all the ingredients together.

Cachumber Palava

YIELDS ABOUT
1 CUP

A simple and colorful chutney. Serve fresh.

INGREDIENTS

2 small red onions, peeled and chopped	1 tablespoon chopped green or purple bell pepper
1 teaspoon chopped fresh cilantro leaves	1/4 lime
1/2 teaspoon dried mint	

METHOD

■ Simply mix all the ingredients together, serving the lime wedge on top.

Cachumber Punjabi

YIELDS ABOUT
1/2 CUP

Another version of the previous recipe.

INGREDIENTS

1/2 Spanish onion, peeled and chopped	1 teaspoon each of chopped red and yellow bell peppers
1 teaspoon chopped fresh cilantro leaves	1 green hot pepper, chopped (optional)

METHOD

■ Simply mix all the ingredients together.

Coconut Chutney

YIELDS ABOUT
1/2 CUP

Originating from South India, but delicious as a chutney with any dish. It's easy to make, and very tasty.

INGREDIENTS

2 teaspoons mustard or peanut oil	1 tablespoon coconut, ground to a powder
2 teaspoons sesame seeds	Milk
1 teaspoon black mustard seeds	Pinch of salt
3 tablespoons flaked coconut	

METHOD

- Heat the oil, and fry the seeds for 1 minute. Cool.

- Mix the two coconuts with enough milk to form a stiff paste. Mix with the spices and salt. Serve cold.

Imli

TAMARIND CHUTNEY

YIELDS ABOUT
3/4 CUP

This is a very tasty chutney—a dip really. Pity that so few restaurants make it, but it does take time to make the tamarind juice.

INGREDIENTS

3/4 cup Tamarind Purée (see page 34)	Salt to taste
Brown sugar to taste	1 teaspoon Curry Paste (storebought or homemade, see page 20)

METHOD

- Simply mix all the ingredients together.

Thai Cucumber

YIELDS ABOUT
2 CUPS

A tangy chutney from Thailand that goes well with Indian food, too.

INGREDIENTS

4-inch piece cucumber, quartered and chopped

1 scallion, trimmed and chopped

1 tablespoon chopped fresh cilantro leaves

1 teaspoon sesame seeds

6–8 tablespoons any vinegar

1 teaspoon white sugar

Salt to taste

METHOD

■ Simply mix all the ingredients together.

White Radish (Mooli) Chutney

YIELDS ABOUT
3 CUPS

Fresh, tangy, and quick to make, this chutney goes well with all dishes.

INGREDIENTS

1 8-inch *mooli* (daikon), about 8 ounces

1 tablespoon white distilled vinegar

1 teaspoon Curry Paste (storebought or homemade, see page 20)

METHOD

■ Wash the *mooli*, scrape the outside clean, and cut off top and bottom. Shred it in a food processor or a grater into thin strips.

■ Mix the vinegar and curry paste, then combine with the *mooli*.

■ Serve cold and fresh. Either freeze any leftovers or cook it into your next curry.

Sag Pachadi

SPINACH CHUTNEY

**SERVES 4
AS A SIDE**

This is a kind of *raita* (a yogurt-based salad) from the southern tip of India. Make it as thick or thin as you like and serve it as an accompaniment, hot or cold.

INGREDIENTS

1 pound fresh spinach (or frozen)	1 1/4 cups plain yogurt, strained
1 tablespoon cumin seeds	Akhni Stock (see page 23) or milk, if necessary
2 tablespoons mustard or peanut oil	
1 tablespoon mustard seeds	

METHOD

- Thoroughly wash the fresh spinach, then coarsely chop it. Boil for 3 minutes and strain. (If using frozen spinach, thaw and chop it; do not boil.)

- Heat a dry pan on the stove and roast the cumin seeds.

- Heat the oil and fry the mustard seeds until they pop. Add the spinach away from the heat, then the yogurt. Heat gently (if you wish to serve the dish hot) and stir frequently to prevent curdling.

- Add the roasted cumin. If you want a runnier dish, simply add stock or milk to the desired consistency.

Mint Raita

YOGURT CHUTNEY

YIELDS ABOUT
1 CUP

A deliciously cool and cooling accompaniment. It should be chilled and served within the hour.

INGREDIENTS

INGREDIENTS	GARNISHES
1 cup plain yogurt	Fresh chopped cilantro
1 teaspoon finely chopped fresh mint	Pinch of nutmeg
Salt and pepper	

SPICES (OPTIONAL)

1/2 teaspoon ground red pepper (cayenne)

1/2 teaspoon Garam Masala (storebought or homemade, see page 35)

METHOD

■ Drain any excess liquid off the yogurt, then beat with a whisk or fork, rotary or electric beater until smooth.

■ Add mint, salt, and pepper plus the **Spices**, if used.

■ Serve chilled within the hour. Garnish before serving with fresh cilantro and nutmeg.

DESSERTS

▲▲▲▲▲▲▲▲▲▲▲▲▲▲▲▲▲▲

The desserts and confections of India are quite frankly very limited in range, and they are an acquired taste. They are usually very sweet indeed, very sticky, and most are milk based.

In this chapter I have reduced the sugar levels to a more acceptable amount (you can always add more), which I find brings out the delightful (once acquired) tastes of the spicing, usually green cardamom and saffron.

I urge you to try Indian desserts from time to time, but if you want something lighter, Indian's national fruit—the mango—is ideal.

Firni

SPICY WHITE CUSTARD

SERVES 4

Firni is typical of the Indian pudding, and it consists of milk, cornstarch, sugar, nuts, and spices. It is served cold. A variation of this recipe is *Faloda*.

INGREDIENTS

4 cups milk	
2 tablespoons cornstarch or rice flour	
1 cup sweetened condensed milk	
1/2 teaspoon ground green cardamom	
2 tablespoons dry milk powder	
2 tablespoons ground almonds	

GARNISHES

Silver or gold leaf (*vark*) (see page 144)
Pistachio nuts, chopped

METHOD

■ Make a paste from a little milk and the cornstarch.

■ Heat the 4 cups of milk, but don't boil it. Add the paste and stir until it thickens.

■ Add all the remaining ingredients and mix in gently.

■ Pour into a decorative serving bowl and place it in the refrigerator for at least 2 hours to thicken.

■ Garnish with silver or gold leaf and pistachio nuts.

Shahi Kheer

CREAMY RICE PUDDING

SERVES 4

Every year in late September a great festival is held all over India to give thanksgiving to Ganesha (the elephant god). A special sweet is prepared and eaten in celebration—*kheer*, basically a creamy rice pudding.

INGREDIENTS

1/2 cup short-grain pudding rice
2 1/4 cups milk
1 cup sweetened condensed milk
1/2 teaspoon saffron

GARNISHES

1 tablespoon golden raisins
1 tablespoon sliced almonds

METHOD

■ Soak the rice in cold water for 30 minutes, then rinse.

■ Boil the rice and the milk together, then simmer, stirring from time to time, until the rice is cooked and soft (about 15 minutes).

■ Add the condensed milk and saffron. When hot, serve garnished with the golden raisins and sliced almonds. It can also be served cold.

Coconut Pancakes

YIELDS 12–14

INGREDIENTS

1 cup white flour
1/4 cup butter, melted
2 eggs, beaten
1 1/4 cups milk, warmed
1 tablespoon sugar
Few drops of vanilla extract
Butter
Lemon juice

FILLING

2 1/2 cups grated fresh coconut
1/4 cup brown sugar
1/4 cup raisins
1/4 teaspoon ground cassia bark or cinnamon
1/4 teaspoon ground green cardamom

METHOD

■ To make the pancakes, sift the flour into a bowl, and mix in the melted butter, eggs, warm milk, sugar, and vanilla. Mix well. It should be of pouring consistency. Mix all the filling ingredients together.

■ In a very hot *tava* or on a heated griddle, heat a little butter. Pour in enough batter which, when swirled around the pan, makes a thin pancake.

■ Place some of the filling in the center of each pancake. Roll up and keep warm. Serve with a squeeze of lemon.

Kesari Shrikhand

SAFFRON YOGURT SYLLABUB

SERVES 4

Shrikhand is incredibly easy to make, as it is virtually instant. It is light and sweet and, being thick in texture, it is fun and elegant to serve it in stemmed wine glasses for the more elaborate occasion. You can reduce the strain of entertaining by putting the mixture into the glasses early and keeping them in the refrigerator until you are ready to serve.

INGREDIENTS

2 1/2 cups plain yogurt, strained (best for taste and texture)

2/3 cup whipping cream

2 tablespoons ground almonds

3 tablespoons sugar (or to taste)

1 teaspoon ground green cardamoms

6–10 saffron strands

GARNISHES

Freshly grated nutmeg

Pistachio nuts, chopped

METHOD

■ Simply hand beat all the ingredients together.

■ After placing into serving bowls or glasses, garnish with freshly grated nutmeg and pistachio nuts.

Shahi Tukre

INDIAN BREAD AND BUTTER PUDDING

SERVES 4

Don't be put off by the thought that this is a soggy, unappealing pudding. It is, in fact, very Indian and when spiced with green cardamom, saffron, vanilla, and rosewater, and garnished with silver leaf (*vark*), it is one of then nicest of Indian puddings. Served cold, it can be made well in advance, which is especially useful if using it for a dinner party, and no one will guess its humble and relatively inexpensive ingredients.

I first met this dish (also called *Double Ka Mitha*) in Delhi, and I have since cooked it several times for up to sixty people. It is quite delicious.

INGREDIENTS

8 slices white sliced bread	1/2 teaspoon ground green cardamoms
Vegetable oil for deep-frying	Few drops of rosewater
4 cups milk	GARNISH
1 cup sweetened condensed milk	1 tablespoon sliced almonds, roasted
1/2 teaspoon saffron	1 tablespoon pistachio nuts, chopped
Few drops of vanilla extract	4 silver or gold leaf sheets (see page 144)

METHOD

■ Remove the crusts from the bread and discard. Deep-fry the bread at 375°F until golden. Remove and drain.

■ Using a nonstick pan (to prevent burning), bring the milk to a boil, then reduce the heat to a simmer. Add the condensed milk and simmer for 15 minutes to thicken it, stirring occasionally.

■ Add the saffron, vanilla, green cardamom, and rosewater, and remove from the heat.

■ Arrange four of the fried bread slices to cover the base of a small baking dish. Place the other slices on top. Pour the milk mixture over the bread, ensuring that the bread is thoroughly soaked.

■ Place the baking dish immediately into an oven preheated to 375°F. Bake for 15 minutes, then take out and cool. It will set firm.

■ When cold, cut into four portions. Place on flat serving plates, and garnish with the nuts and the silver or gold leaf. Place in the refrigerator until ready to serve.

Kulfi

INDIAN ICE CREAM

YIELDS 10

The concept of ice cream in India is by no means a modern one. Long before the advent of refrigerators and freezers, *kulfi* was being made successfully. It probably started in its present form at the time of the Moghul emperors, for it is known that every day a huge load of ice was dispatched from the Punjabi hills to the emperors to ensure they always had chilled water, and no doubt *kulfi*, no matter where they were or whatever the temperature. (The emperors only drank water from the River Ganges, and it was collected and sent each day!)

This recipe requires the milk to be reduced—a lengthy process requiring very frequent stirring to prevent the milk from burning. Traditionally *kulfi* is frozen in conical molds—exactly the same shape as our ice cream cones. If you do not have this shape on hand, use small yogurt containers.

INGREDIENTS

5 quarts whole milk	1/2 cup chopped nuts (almond, cashew and pistachio)
1 1/4 cups sugar	
1/2 teaspoon ground green cardamoms	Few drops rosewater

METHOD

- Using a wok, *karahi*, or large saucepan—preferably with a nonstick surface—bring the milk to the boiling point, then reduce the temperature to a simmer.

- Stir frequently until the milk reduces to a thick consistency (like condensed milk) when it is called *khoya*. This is tedious and can take a very long time—an hour or more.

- Remove from the stove and add the remaining ingredients (omit the nuts if you do not like that texture).

- Place the mixture into *kulfi* molds or yogurt containers, and freeze.

- To serve, remove from the molds, and garnish with more chopped nuts.

Moira Banana

SERVES 4

In the state of Goa there is a town called Moira. It is not a place where tourists go, and it is unremarkable in many ways. But from that town I collected this deliciously simple recipe, which uses a particular kind of local banana. This is not exported, but I have found it works well with ordinary bananas.

INGREDIENTS

2 tablespoons raisins	2 tablespoons butter ghee
2 tablespoons golden raisins	4 tablespoons brown sugar
1 tablespoon chopped mixed nuts	2 tablespoons sherry or rum
Water	4 large fresh bananas

METHOD

■ Grind the raisins, golden raisins, and nuts in a food processor with a little water.

■ Heat the ghee with an equal quantity of water. Add the sugar and stir well. When simmering, add the raisins, golden raisins, and nuts. Simmer for a while so that it thickens a little. Add the sherry or rum, then remove from the heat.

■ Peel and chop the bananas. Pour the hot sauce over them and serve at once.

Fresh Fruit Sorbet

SERVES 4

Modern India has quickly learned the art of sorbet making, and it is a tasty way of enjoying exotic fruit, and goes especially well after the contrasting spicy tastes of curry. You can control the amount of sugar to achieve very tart or sweet tastes, whichever you prefer, and the fruit can be anything that is available.

INGREDIENTS

1/2 cup granulated sugar	Juice of 1 lemon
1 1/4 cups water	1 egg white
12 ounces fruit, after de-skinning, seeding, and puréeing	

METHOD

■ Place the sugar and water in a saucepan and bring to a simmer. Continue simmering and stirring until the mixture becomes tacky.

■ Remove from the heat and allow to cool.

■ Add the puréed fruit and the lemon juice. Mix well, then freeze for exactly 1 hour.

■ Whip the egg white so that it is firm enough to form stiff peaks. Fold into the cold fruit, and freeze again for at least 24 hours.

■ To serve, use an ice-cream scoop.

GLOSSARY

Included in this glossary is an explanation of some of the spices used in the recipes in this book.

A

Allspice Native to the West Indies. Related to the clove family, the seed resembles small dried peas. Called allspice because its aroma seems to combine those of clove, cinnamon, ginger, nutmeg, and pepper. Used rather more in Middle Eastern cooking than Indian.
Am Chur Mango powder.
Aniseed *Saunf.* Small deliciously flavored seeds resembling fennel seeds.
Asfoetida *Hing.* Gum obtained from root of giant fennel-like plant. Used in powder of resin form. A rather smelly spice.
Ata or *Atta* (*Chupatti*) flour. Fine whole-grain flour used in most Indian breads. Whole-wheat flour is a suitable alternative.

B

Basmati The best type of long-grain rice.
Bay leaf This very well-known leaf is used fresh or dried in certain Indian recipes.
Besan. See chickpea flour
Blachan. See Shrimp Paste

C

Cardamom *Elaichi.* One of the most aromatic and expensive spices. It is a pod containing slightly sticky black seeds. There are three main types: Brown (also called black) have a rather hairy, husky, dark brown casing about 3/4 inch long. Used in garam masala, *kormas,* and pullaos. Quite pungent Green have a smooth, pale green outer casing about 1/3 inch long. Used whole or ground, with or without casing in many savory and sweet recipes. White are about the same size as green with a slightly rounder, white casing. Green and white have a similar flavor—more delicate than the brown.

Cassia bark A corky bark with a sweet fragrance similar to cinnamon. Cassia is coarser and cooks better than cinnamon and is used extensively in northern Indian cooking. Although cooked in the curry, the bark is too coarse to eat.
Chana Type of lentil. See *dhal.*
Chickpea flour *Besan.* Finely ground flour, pale blonde in color, made from *chana* (see *Dhal*). Used to make *pakoras* and to thicken curries.
Cilantro. See Coriander
Cinnamon *Dalchini.* The quill-like dried bark of the cinnamon tree. It is one of the most aromatic spices. Same family as cassia, it is generally used in dishes that require a delicate flavor.
Cloves *Lavang.* A familiar spice in the West where it has been continuously used since

Roman times. Expensive and fragrant, it is an unopened flower bud.

Coriander *Dhania* (also called **Cilantro** when the leaves are used). One of the most important spices in Indian cooking. The leaves of the plant (cilantro) can be used fresh and the seeds used whole or ground.

Cumin *Jeera*. There are two types of seeds: white and black. The white seeds are a very important spice in Indian cooking. The black seeds (*kala jeera*) are nice in *pullao* rice and certain vegetable dishes. Both can be used whole or ground.

Curry The only word in this glossary to have no direct translation into any of the sub-continent's fifteen or so languages. The word was coined by the British in India centuries ago. Possible contenders for the origin of the word are *karahi* or *karai* (Hindi), a wok-like frying pan used all over India to prepare masalas (spice mixtures), *karhi*, a soup-like dish made with spices, chickpea flour dumplings, and buttermilk, *kair*, a spicy Tamil sauce, *Turkuri*, a seasoned sauce or stew, or *karai phulia*, neem or curry leaves. *Kudhi* or *kadhi*, a yogurt soup, or *koresh*, an aromatic Iranian stew.

Curry leaves Neem leaves or *kari phulia*. Small leaves a bit like bay leaves, used for flavoring.

D

Dhal Lentils and beans. There are over sixty types of lentils in the sub-continent, some of which are very obscure. Like peas, they grow into a hard sphere measuring between 1/3 inch (chickpeas) and 3/100 inch (*urid*). They are cooked whole or split with skin, or split with it polished off. Lentils are a rich source of protein and when cooked with spices are extremely tasty. The common types of *chana* (resembling yellow split peas, used to make chickpea flour/*besan*; *kabli chana* (chickpeas); *masoor* (the most familiar orangey-red lentil which has a green skin); *moong* (green skin lentil, used also to make bean sprouts); *toot*, or *toovar* (dark yellow and very oily); and *urid* (black skin, white lentil).

Dhania Coriander.

F

Fennel *Sonf* or *soonf*. A small green seed which is very aromatic, with aniseed taste. Delicious in *pullao* rice.

Fenugreek *Methi*. This important spice is used as seeds and in fresh or dried leaf form. It is very savory and is used in many Northern Indian dishes.

Fish sauce *Nam-pla* (Thai), *Ngapya* (Burmese), *Patis* (Philippine). It is the runny liquid strained from fermented anchovies, and is a very important flavoring agent.

Five spice powder Combination of five sweet and aromatic spices used in Chinese and Malay cooling. Usually ground. A typical combination would be equal parts of cinnamon, cloves, fennel seeds, star anise, and Szechuan pepper.

G

Galangal A tuber related to ginger which comes in varieties called greater or lesser. It has a more peppery flavor than ginger (which can be substituted for it). It is used in Thai cooking, where it is called *kha*, and in Indonesian (*laos*) and Malay (*kenkur*). It is available in fresh form (rare), dried, or powdered.

Garam masala Literally "hot mixture." This refers to a blend of spices much loved in northern Indian cooking.

Ghee Clarified butter or margarine much used in northern Indian cooking.

Ginger *Adrak* (fresh). *Sont* (dried), a rhizome that can be used fresh, dried, or powdered.

Gosht Lamb, mutton, or goat.

H

Hot peppers There are a great many species of chiles, which are the fleshy pods of the shrub-like bushes of the capsicum family.

Chiles range from large to small, and colors include green, white, purple, pink, and red. Curiously, although synonymous with Indian food they were only brought to the subcontinent from South America some four centuries ago. They are now the most important heat agent in Indian cooking. They vary in hotness from mild to incendiary-like potency. Most commonly, small green or red hot peppers are used fresh. Red hot peppers can be dried and used whole, and ground red pepper is made by grinding dried cayenne pepper.

Huldi Turmeric.

J

Jeera or *Zeera* Cumin.

K

Kabli chana Chickpeas. See *Dhal.*
Kalongi See wild onion seeds
Karahi *Karai, korai,* etc. Cast-iron or steel wok-like frying or serving pan. Some restaurants cook in small *karahis* and serve them straight to the table with the food sizzling inside.

L

Lemongrass *Takrai* (Thai), *serai* (Malay). A fragrant leafed plant that imparts a subtle lemony flavor to cooking. Use ground powder (made from the bulb) as a substitute.
Lentils see *Dhal.*
Lime leaves *Markrut* or citrus leaves. Used in Thai cooking—fresh or dried—to give a distinctive aromatic flavor.
Lovage *Ajwainz* or *ajowain.* Slightly bitter round seeds.

M

Mango Powder *Am Chur.* A very sour flavoring agent.
Masala A mixture of spices which are cooked with a particular dish. Any curry powder is therefore a masala. It can be spelled a remarkable number of ways—*massala, massalla, musala, mosola, massalam,* etc.

Masoor Red lentils. See *Dhal.*
Methi Fenugreek.
Mirch Pepper or chile.
Moglai or *Moghlai* Cooking in the style of the Moghul emperors whose chefs took Indian cooking to the heights of gourmet cuisine three centuries ago. Few restaurateurs who offer Moglai dishes come anywhere near this excellence. True Moglai dishes are expensive and time-consuming to prepare authentically. Can also be variously spelled *muglai, mhogulai, moghlai,* etc.
Moong Type of lentil. See *Dhal.*
Mustard seed Small black seeds which become sweetish when fried. Yellow variety used to make English mustard to which flour and coloring is added.

N

Nam Pla Fish sauce.
Nga-Pi Shrimp paste
Nga-Pya Fish sauce.
Nigella Wild onion seed.

P

Pappadam Thin lentil flour wafers. When cooked (deep-fried or baked) they expand to about 8 inches. They must be crackling crisp and warm when served. They come plain or spiced with lentils, pepper, garlic, or hot pepper. Many spelling variations include *popodon, pappodon,* etc.
Paprika Mild red ground pepper made from red capsicum peppers. It originally came from Hungary and only reached India this century. Its main use is to give red color to a dish.
Patna A long-grained rice.
Pepper *Mirch.* Has for centuries been India's most important spice, gaining it the title "king of spices." It grows on vines which flower triennially and produce clusters of berries, which are picked and dried and become the peppercorns. Green, black, and white pepper are not different varieties. All peppercorns are green when picked and must be bottled or freeze-dried at once to retain the color. Black pepper

169

is the dried berry. White pepper is obtained by soaking off the black skin of the berry. Peppercorns are a heat agent and can be used whole or ground.

Pistachio nut *Pista magaz.* A fleshy, tasty nut which can be used fresh (the greener the better) or salted. It is expensive and goes well in savory or sweet dishes such as *biriani* or *pista kulfi* (ice cream).

Poppy seed *Cus cus.* White seeds used to thicken curries; blue seeds used to decorate bread. Not to be con fused with the Moroccan national dish—couscous—made from steamed semolina.

S

Saffron *Kesar* or *zafron.* The world's most expensive spice, saffron is the stigma of the crocus flower. A few stigmas are all that are needed to give a recipe a delicate yellow coloring and aroma.

Sesame seed *Til.* Small round disks, the white species are widely used in Indian cooking, the black in Chinese.

Shrimp paste *Blachau* (Malay), *nga-pi* (Burmese), *kapi* (Thai). Very concentrated block of compressed shrimp. A vital flavorer for the cooking of those countries.

Star Anise A pretty star-shaped spice used in Chinese five spices, and it is lovely in *pullao* rice.

Sub-continent Term to describe India, Pakistan, Bangladesh, Nepal, Burma, and Sri Lanka as a group.

Supari Mixture of seeds and sweeteners for chewing after a meal. Usually includes aniseed or fennel, shredded betel nut, sugar balls, squash seeds, etc.

T

Tamarind *Imli.* A date-like fruit used as a chutney, and in cooking as a souring agent (see page 34).

Tej Patia The leaf of the cassia bark tree. Resembles bay leaf, which can be used in its place.

Thali A tray which holds the complete meal served in individual bowls (*katori*). Used by diners in the south.

Toor* or *Toovar Type of lentil. See *Dhal.*

Turmeric *Haldi* or *huldi.* A very important Indian spice, turmeric is a rhizome. The fresh root is used occasionally as a vegetable or in pickles. The ground spice is extensively used to give the familiar yellow color to curries. Use sparingly or it can cause bitterness.

U

Urid A type of lentil. See *Dhal.*

V

Vark* or *Varak Edible silver or gold foil. See page 144.

W

Wild Onion Seed *Kalongi.* Small irregular jet-black nuggets that have an oniony fragrance though they are not from an onion species. Also known as *Nigella.*

INDEX

COOKBOOKS BY THE CROSSING PRESS

Homestyle Chinese Cooking
By Yan-kit So

These delicious recipes include the six primary ways in which the Wok may be used, from Soups, Steaming, and Stir-frying, to Sautéing, Deep-frying, and Braising.
$16.95 • Paper • ISBN 0-89594-883-4

Homestyle Italian Cooking
By Lori Carangelo

These wonderful dishes use fresh ingredients, carefully prepared to bring out the special flavors of the best, homestyle Italian cooking.
$16.95 • Paper • ISBN 0-89594-867-2

Homestyle Mexican Cooking
By Lourdes Nichols

This tantalizing collection of over 180 authentic recipes from Mexican cuisine includes meat and poultry dishes and recipes for rice dishes, vegetables, salads, desserts, and drinks.
$16.95 • Paper • ISBN 0-89594-861-3

Homestyle Middle Eastern Cooking
By Pat Chapman

This collection of authentic recipes features spicy regional dishes selected from hundreds of recipes the author collected on his travels throughout the Middle East.
$16.95 • Paper • ISBN 0-89594-860-5

Homestyle Southeast Asian Cooking
By Rani King and Chandra Khan

Well-traveled sisters show you how to recreate their favorite recipes so that you too can enjoy the many exquiste flavors and taste sensations from the exotic lands of Sri Lanka, Thailand, Malaysia, and Indonesia.
$16.95 • Paper • ISBN 0-89594-905-9

Homestyle Thai and Indonesian Cooking
By Sri Owen

Sri Owen offers authentic recipes for satés, curries, fragrant rice dishes, spicy vegetables, and snacks and sweets. Includes adaptations using Western ingredients.
$16.95 • Paper • ISBN 0-89594-859-1

COOKBOOKS BY THE CROSSING PRESS

SPECIALTY SERIES

Biscotti, Bars, and Brownies
By Terri Henry
$6.95 • Paper • ISBN 0-89594-901-6

Old World Breads
By Charel Scheele
$6.95 • Paper • ISBN 0-89594-902-4

Quick Breads
By Howard Early and Glenda Morris
$6.95 • Paper • ISBN 0-89594-941-5

Salad Dressings
By Teresa H. Burns
$6.95 • Paper • ISBN 0-89594-895-8

Sun-Dried Tomatoes
By Andrea Chesman
$6.95 • Paper • ISBN 0-89594-900-8

Wholesome Cookies
By Jane Marsh Dieckman
$6.95 • Paper • ISBN 0-89594-942-3

OTHER COOKBOOKS

The Low Fat Vegetarian Cookbook
By Sue Kreitzman
$14.95 • Paper • ISBN 0-89594-834-6

International Vegetarian Cooking
By Judy Ridgway
$14.95 • Paper • ISBN 0-89594-854-0

Japanese Vegetarian Cooking
By Patricia Richfield
$14.95 • Paper • ISBN 0-89594-805-2

Cooking the Fat Free, Salt Free, Sugar-Free, Flavor-Full Way
By Marcia Sabate Williams
$22.95 • Paper • ISBN 0-89594-858-3

Marinades
By Jim Tarantino
$16.95 • Paper • 0-89594-531-2

Balanced Diet Cookbook:
By Bill Taylor
$16.95 • Paper • 0-89594-874-5

To receive a current catalog from The Crossing Press
please call toll-free,
800-777-1048.
Visit our Web site on the Internet: www. crossingpress.com